Park Ranger Guide to Wildlife

Park Ranger Guide to Wildlife

Arthur P. Miller, Jr.

Drawings by David Besenger

PARK RANGER GUIDES

STACKPOLE BOOKS

Published by
STACKPOLE BOOKS
Cameron and Kelker Streets
P.O. Box 1831
Harrisburg, PA 17105

Printed in the United States of America

Cover photo © John Colwell/Grant Heilman Photography, Inc.

Cover design by Tracy Patterson.

Interior design by Marcia Lee Dobbs.

Photography by Arthur P. Miller, Jr.

Library of Congress Cataloging-in-Publication Data

Miller, Arthur P., Jr.
    Park ranger guide to wildlife / Arthur P. Miller, Jr. : line
drawings by David Besenger.
        p.   cm.
    ISBN 0-8117-2289-9
    1. Wildlife watching—United States—Guide books. I. Title.
QL60.M55   1990
335.95'4'0973—dc20   89-39934
                                                   CIP

Contents

Introduction

"At noon the plain before us was alive with thousands of buffalo—bulls, cows, and calves," wrote Francis Parkman, a young adventurer, in 1846 on his first buffalo hunt in Colorado. "The swelling prairie was darkened with them to the very horizon," he noted.

No longer do vast herds of bison thunder across the Great Plains. Nor do elk graze in the mid-Atlantic and southeastern United States, as they once did, though they are still found in the West.

As development spread across the country, farmers cut into forests to open fields for crops. Canals, highways, and railroads crisscrossed the wilderness. Factories grew along riverbanks, then moved inland. Wild animals retreated. Trappers' snares and hunters' guns took their toll until angry conservationists called for a halt to the slaughter.

At the turn of the century the federal government stepped in to preserve the nation's magnificent scenic wonders and its variety of wild animals, setting aside national parks, wildlife refuges, and national forests. Within these preserves animals still live in their natural habitats and Americans can observe their wildlife heritage.

In these wilderness enclaves animals live and die. They mark off territory, forage for food, prey and are preyed upon, sleep, hibernate, reproduce, and rear their young.

Visitors have the privilege of entering this wild world to admire the grace and beauty of untamed creatures and marvel at the ingenious ways they cope with their environment. Many of us have a desire to interact with the creatures whose land we share. We thrill to see for the first time an animal we have known only as a picture in a book.

None could be better suited to introduce us to these wild animals than the park rangers, biologists, and wildlife specialists who serve in refuges, national parks, and national forests. The only problem is that these specialists are too busy managing their sanctuaries to write a book.

In my fourteen years as a public affairs director in the National Park Service, I discovered that the traveling public had more questions about wild animals than we had ready answers. Where, they asked, could they see a bison? How many bears are there in Shenandoah National Park? When does a mule deer shed its antlers? Are whooping cranes extinct?

This book will answer those questions, providing a guide to the better places to view animals in the wild. Those closest to the animals—the rangers—share their knowledge about the best ways to observe wildlife in its native habitat.

To gather facts for this book, my wife Marge and I interviewed more than a hundred rangers, biologists, resource managers, naturalists, interpreters, guides, researchers, refuge managers, park superintendents, and forest supervisors. Their firsthand knowledge of mammals, amphibians, reptiles, and birds of prey brings authenticity to these pages.

As we walked the trails and tracked animals, we talked with rangers, who were eager to share their knowledge. They would like visitors to better understand and appreciate their wildlife heritage.

To Marge, who shared the twelve thousand miles of travel that revealed the remarkable diversity of wild animals in this country, I am indebted for much of the interviewing and research. To all those along the way who shared their experiences, laid out our path, and patiently read the manuscript, we are deeply grateful. And for the animals themselves we retain a full measure of admiration.

CHAPTER 1

The Animals
Around Us

Across the flat grassland we saw them: a herd of about fifty bison, dark brown bulks against the tan prairie grass of Badlands National Park in South Dakota. Pulling our motor home over to the shoulder of the park road, we got out to watch.

It was the fall mating season, or rut, and consequently the bulls had joined the cows and calves. During the rest of the year each bull stakes out its own territory and forages for itself. Through binoculars Marge and I singled out a group of three bison—a cow, a bull, and a calf probably less than a year old.

The bull followed the cow step for step, snorting as it grazed. It had evidently selected the cow as its mate and would now "tend" her for several days, accompanying the cow and calf as they moved about the prairie.

As we watched, the three moved along side by side, cropping the grass as they went. Every so often the calf moved to the rear of the cow and tried to nurse. The cow gently kicked the calf away, seemingly not wanting to be bothered. The calf grazed for a while, then made another try for mother's milk, only to be rebuffed.

As we watched the grazing herd, another car pulled onto the shoulder behind us. The couple inside told us they were from Boston. Never, they said, had they experienced such a day. They had seen a herd of pronghorn in the morning and had watched the bustling activity at a prairie dog town at noon before discovering this bison herd. It had been a banner day of wildlife watching for them—and for us.

It is stimulating to discover the diversity of the wild animal world. From microbes, the smallest known life forms, to the blue whale, the largest, millions of species of wildlife inhabit the earth. Zoologists have classified some six thousand species of mammals, sixty-five hundred reptiles, and twenty-five hundred amphibians, not to mention the whole panoply of fish, birds, and insects. In North America alone live some four hundred species of mammals.

Animals come in many shapes and sizes. They walk, run, crawl, hop, burrow, fly in the air, and swim in the water. Remarkably, each kind of animal is different from every other one. Each is especially suited to the place where it lives and the food it eats. Each pursues its own way of life within the constraints of its environment.

Even though much of the United States has been plowed under, industrialized, mined, or developed, there remain many pockets of wilderness where wild animals can thrive. For the wildlife seeker, our national parks, national wildlife refuges, national forests and public lands, state parks and game lands, county parks—even military bases and utility properties—offer opportunities to view wildlife ranging from bobcats to bison, from the small pika to the speedy pronghorn, from the one-half-ounce field mouse to the one thousand-pound moose.

Fascinating insights await the observer in this world of wild animals. A group of visitors enjoying a picnic lunch one day at Wind Cave National Park in South Dakota got a rare look at the interdependence of animals, thanks to Bill Swift, the chief of interpretation for the park.

Just as Bill stopped to chat with the visitors, a mule deer emerged from the forest to browse on low tree branches and shrubs at the edge of the clearing. When the picnickers noticed the deer, Bill explained that deer often browse along the forest edge and suggested that everyone simply continue what they were doing and learn what they could of mule deer behavior.

"Little did I guess what we would witness," Bill later told us. It turned out to be a once-in-a-lifetime episode, even for a veteran naturalist like Bill.

A magpie flew out of a tree and landed on the deer's back. The muley paid no attention. The magpie then made its way along the deer's back until it reached one of the animal's large ears. (It is these large ears, like the mule's, that give the deer its name.) The bird then proceeded to pluck lice and bugs from the deer's ear. The deer continued to browse, allowing the magpie to groom it.

The unusual incident gave Bill Swift an opportunity to explain to the visitors the natural phenomenon of mutualism, a form of symbiosis or social contract that binds different species to each other. "I'm not sure these folks fully realized what a rare and exciting privilege they shared with me that day," he said.

Park rangers like Bill Swift use these experiences to emphasize some of the basic concepts of nature. As they conduct nature hikes and give campfire talks, they discuss the natural principles important to an understanding of animals in the wild.

During rutting season, a bull bison (left) and a young calf (center) vie for a cow's attention at Badlands National Park in South Dakota. The calf, not yet weaned, tries to nurse from its mother, only to be shoved aside by the courting adults.

Balance of nature. This principle says that plants and animals remain relatively constant in numbers. Natural enemies prevent an animal species from becoming so numerous that it upsets the balance. Should a population become too large, some of the animals die from lack of food or from disease.

The balance-of-nature principle also embraces the cycle of growth and decay. Simple chemical substances become living things and living things in turn break down into simple chemicals. Animals, for example, eat and thereby destroy plants. But the animal puts chemicals back into the soil in the form of body wastes, which act as fertilizer for new plants. When an animal or a plant dies, it decays. This process returns to the soil chemicals that aid in new growth and life.

How animals adapt to their environment. Over many years of evolution animals have adapted to their respective environments in order to survive. Camouflage, or protective coloration, is the main means of protection for some. Thus, animals of the desert are generally pale or earth-colored compared to forest dwellers of the same species.

Animals cope with cold weather in different ways. Some, like the coyote, simply "tough it out," relying on a warm fur coat to keep its body temperature high enough. Rodents and other animals burrow beneath the ground to get below the snow and freezing temperatures. Others hibernate, sleeping through much of the winter. Hibernators exert little energy, living off the body fat they store up during warm-weather months. Still others, such as birds of prey, migrate to other regions where it is warmer.

Many animals inhabit a territory.   Most animals claim a territory, or home range, in which they live and seek food. Bears, mountain lions, and wolves patrol hunting territories up to fifty miles wide. A field mouse, on the other hand, may never venture more than fifty feet from its door. Each animal comes to know its home range thoroughly—good food sources, escape routes to use when predators threaten, good nesting sites. When a fox chases a rabbit, the rabbit may run to the edge of its territory, then turn and run along the boundary line so as not to trespass on another rabbit's turf. Territories ensure that too many animals will not crowd into an area and deplete the food supply, creating greater competition between animals.

Wild animals versus domesticated animals.   Wild animals—the great majority of the animal kingdom—are those that man has not domesticated.

Early man hunted animals for food. He probably first tamed the dog and used it to help him hunt other animals. Some twelve thousand years ago, historians say, he captured and tamed cattle, goats, and sheep for additional meat to eat. He succeeded in domesticating the pig about eight thousand years ago. Man first tamed the horse for its meat also, but later learned to use it to ride, to carry his burdens, and to pull loads.

He selected certain animals and bred them over many generations, producing the characteristics he desired. He put these animals to use as pack carriers, givers of milk, suppliers of meat, and providers of blood, furs, and hides. When early explorers settled new continents, they took their animals with them, spreading their domesticated animals to new regions.

Wild animals, on the other hand, have never been domesticated. They live in habitats that best suit them, occupying a territory and often defending it from other animals. They forage or seek the prey they need to survive, respond to seasonal changes in their environment, and reproduce through natural selection.

Feral animals are neither truly wild nor truly domesticated. Like the wild horses of the western lands and the wild hogs of the Great Smoky Mountains, they were once domesticated but have since reverted to the wild state.

But anyone interested in wildlife need not go to the Great Smoky Mountains to observe these principles of nature. More than likely, you can see them at work in your own backyard, or in your city or county park.

Wildlife Close to Home

You can learn a lot about wild animals and increase your powers of observation through experiences close to home. Even the view from your kitchen may provide a good window on local wildlife.

At my home in Pennsylvania a grove of walnut trees provides a perpetual food source for a platoon of gray squirrels. We watch as an agile squirrel scurries down a tree from its nest of leaves up high, finds a walnut, and carries it away to bury. On the ground the squirrel runs in quick bursts of speed, stopping occasionally to turn its head from side to side, smelling the wind and peering about. When it leaps to a branch, its long tail acts as a counterbalance in the same way that a pole is used by a high-wire performer to steady himself.

During winter I have watched a squirrel hunt for the nuts it has carefully set aside in fall. How does it find its buried treasure? Some biologists used to think it was by memory. Recent research, however, concludes that the squirrel finds its way back to the buried nuts by its keen sense of smell. When snow covers the ground, I have seen a squirrel run across the surface, stop and sniff, then start digging. Within minutes it comes up with a buried nut and a winter meal.

Disguised by its surroundings and alert to an intruder, a dainty sika deer peers from the forest at Chincoteague National Wildlife Refuge in Virginia.

I don't mind a squirrel gathering up dozens of nuts—even if it does leave bits of walnut shell all over the yard—but other activities of the gray squirrel can rub a homeowner the wrong way.

During mating season, a squirrel looks for a safe place to build its nest and rear its young. In an urban or suburban setting this search may end inside a warm building.

That happened at Marge's office. Squirrels gnawed through wooden siding under the eaves to gain entrance to an attic. Once inside they scurried up and down the walls, even gnawing through electrical wiring and two-by-four studs to clear a path to their nesting sites. It took a team of exterminators several visits to rid the office of the squirrels and stop any further structural damage from the squirrel homemaking.

Some wildlife populations are increasing their foraging territories, overlapping into suburban and urban areas. Today white-tailed deer and Canada geese are commonplace in many settled areas where they were not found fifty years ago.

Attract Wildlife to Your Yard

You may be able to encourage some of these animals to come to your backyard if you provide the food, protective cover, and water they need. With appropriate habitat, many animals adapt to living around people.

A bird feeder might attract birds. Thick stands of bushes or shrubbery will provide good cover for rabbits. Chipmunks can find a homesite in a rock wall.

One wildlife enthusiast who lives on ten acres of land in New England reports that by allowing the grass and weeds to grow in his meadow and by leaving piles of brush near the tree line, he has attracted white-tailed deer, wild turkeys, ruffed grouse, woodchucks, raccoons, wood ducks, rabbits, squirrels, skunks, foxes, and several kinds of hawks, owls, and songbirds.

Providing a backyard habitat for wildlife can earn you a certificate from the National Wildlife Federation. This conservation organization encourages its members to provide food, shelter, and protective cover for birds and small mammals. You can get helpful hints on the best trees and shrubs to attract wildlife by writing to the National Wildlife Federation, 1412 16th Street N.W., Washington, DC 20036.

Visit a Local Park

Another way to observe the animals around you is to explore a nearby pond, field, or neighborhood park. There are more than twenty-six thousand state, county, and city parks in the country. Choose the early morning or early evening hours when it is most likely that animals will be foraging. Keep your eyes open for movement and your ears alert for noises. Be ready to stop and remain motionless—an animal that sees no movement on your part may be willing to continue its activity or even approach you more closely.

Join a Nature Center

Consider joining a local nature center. Community-oriented nature centers exist in many metropolitan and rural areas. They are usually privately financed, non-profit organizations that have been established by civic-minded individuals devoted to the conservation of nature.

Most nature centers and their staffs work closely with primary and secondary schools and universities in their area, presenting programs and projects that teachers use to fulfill their state's requirements for environmental education. A youngster in your family may already have benefited from involvement with a nature center.

If not, it might be a good idea to get a family membership. A nature center may offer nature hikes, illustrated talks, workshops, exhibits, and field trips for its members. Opportunities may be available to sharpen wildlife observation skills through a workshop on animal tracking, a class on the signs that animals leave behind them, or a field trip to observe the animals around the center.

Spend some time with knowledgeable members of the nature center staff to pick up animal lore. If the center has an animal blind, use it for observation. Take advantage of weekend field trips. Learning the tricks of the trade while close to home will pay dividends when you take to the field for wildlife watching in earnest.

In forest preserves surrounding Chicago, for example, teachers team up with staff members to help children get acquainted with beavers, muskrats, weasels, foxes, raccoons, great horned owls, deer, and wild turkeys—all within minutes of downtown Chicago.

Visit a Zoo

Zoos are excellent places to see firsthand the animals you hope to see in the wild. Visiting a zoo becomes a dress rehearsal for your expedition to the wilderness.

Most zoos exhibit a variety of mammals, birds, reptiles, and amphibians from the United States and other parts of the world.

These animals, of course, are in an environment controlled by man. Unlike wild animals, the animals in a zoo do not forage for their food, roam free, or defend themselves from predators.

Nevertheless, a zoo provides a splendid chance to observe wild species of animals. You can judge an animal's size, see its color, and learn its distinctive markings—traits you can store in your memory against the day you will try to spot the same animal in its natural background.

You also may study the actions and reactions of the

animals within the constraints of their enclosures. Zoos have made great strides in recent years in presenting animals to the public in settings that come close to duplicating their natural surroundings.

Zoos often display wildlife of their own regions as well as exotic animals of the world. In Audubon Park and Zoological Garden in New Orleans, for example, rare white alligators, cougars, red foxes, black bears, otters, and armadillos live in a re-created cypress swamp.

The Minnesota Zoo near Minneapolis-St. Paul features native fish, wolverines, weasels, fishers, pumas, lynx, and a world-renowned beaver colony. The Arizona-Sonora Desert Museum in Tucson demonstrates how wildlife can exist in a desert environment and enables visitors to see in daylight animals that ordinarily venture out only after dark.

At still other zoos you walk into blackness to see animals that forage at night. Nocturnal animals in the wild are difficult to observe. Even experienced wildlife watchers rarely see animals such as bobcats, owls, or badgers, which patrol their beats under cover of darkness. By fooling the animals into thinking it is nighttime, the zoo gives its visitors a unique opportunity to see these creatures.

For youthful members of your family who will be going on your wildlife expedition, you might suggest that they check out the children's section that many zoos have established. At America's first zoo in Philadelphia, for example, there is a building called "Treehouse" where children learn what it is like to exist as various animals. Giant lifelike fiberglass sculptures of living things and their environments—from bees and their honeycombs to dinosaurs, frog eggs, and a butterfly cocoon—give children the illusion that they have shrunk to the size of the flora and fauna around them. Youngsters can crawl into a beaver lodge, climb inside an egg, or peer through the bulbous eyes of a frog to see what the frog sees. They can even hear and smell some animal sounds and odors.

Zoos also play an important role in the protection and propagation of endangered species. Animals whose numbers have dwindled are transported to the safety of zoos. Here they are bred in captivity. When the number of collected animals increases, some are released back into their native habitat.

By these methods zoos in Europe have saved Père David's deer and the European bison. These two species, now extinct in the wild because of overhunting and loss of habitat, have been preserved in European zoos.

These are ways, then, that you can get acquainted with wild animals before you seek them in their natural habitat. Knowing something about their appearance and characteristics will help you recognize and appreciate the animals you discover in the wild.

CHAPTER 2

Where
Wildlife Awaits You

As I drove the tour road through Merritt Island National Wildlife Refuge in Florida, a raccoon slipped out of the tall marsh grass and scurried onto the road in front of me.

Running on spindly legs in a characteristic loping manner, it seemed to provide a special escort. I slowed my car to stay behind it. After a hundred yards or so my uninvited trailblazer dodged off the road and disappeared back into the high grass.

I continued, admiring the many other species of wildlife protected in this refuge, which is actually part of Cape Canaveral's busy space center. Shore and wading birds, including ducks, egrets, and herons, inhabit its lagoons, marshes, and palmetto groves. Merritt Island harbors more endangered and threatened species than any refuge outside of Hawaii, among them the alligator, manatee, bald eagle, wood stork, peregrine falcon, and several kinds of marine turtles.

Scattered across the United States are hundreds of similar natural preserves where wild animals still roam free. Many are federal preserves, land set aside specifically to protect wildlife and plants, places of scenic beauty, or historic sites; others are forest areas, grazing lands, river corridors, or lakes. Still others are parts of military bases.

State, county, and city parks add to this checkerboard of undeveloped open space. So do state fish and game lands, state forests, and privately owned preserves.

These are the pockets of open space that remain after four centuries of economic growth. The result is quite different from the unpeopled land that greeted the first explorers to reach North America in the sixteenth century.

Francisco Vasquez de Coronado, the Spanish explorer who led an expedition through the Southwest in

1540, wrote of the mountain goats, cougars, wildcats, and flocks of wild turkeys that provided food for his hungry troops.

Settlers on the East Coast found deer, wild turkey, geese, ducks, and shellfish plentiful enough to provide them with bounteous Thanksgiving dinners.

To the north, French explorers like Samuel de Champlain were lured into the Great Lakes region and upper Mississippi River by plentiful beaver. Beaver pelts, shipped to England and France, found a ready market for fashionable men's felt hats.

In these early days of settlement, bison herds extended into the eastern and southern woodlands of America. In 1693 one report told of several bison being killed for meat by French hunters in Florida.

Commercial hunters and trappers soon overplayed their hands. In the year 1626 alone, the Dutch West India Company shipped to Europe thousands of beaver skins, otter skins, mink, wildcat, and muskrat. In South Carolina, traders shipped fifty-four thousand deerskins to England one year. Deer disappeared from Massachusetts so rapidly that the colony as early as 1694 imposed a closed season on hunters.

As settlers crossed the Allegheny Mountains and moved westward in search of farmland and pasture, they found the woods full of game and the rivers and lakes teeming with fish. To feed and protect their families they killed turkeys, waterfowl, bears, bobcats, mountain lions, deer, squirrels, raccoons, and opossums.

By Conestoga wagon and flatboat they came, rolling back the frontier. They dug canals to extend the river systems and built roads to make wagon travel easier.

Settling the land and turning forests into fields cut into much of the wildlife habitat, however. The animals were pushed back and deprived of food, cover, and places to raise their young.

Moreover, the settler, busy building his cabin and plowing his land, had little patience with animals that got in his way. One of these "pests" was the passenger pigeon, a bird that gathered in great flocks and ate the farmer's seed corn.

The farmers cut down many of the hardwood forests where the passenger pigeons nested and killed literally thousands of the birds for food or simply for sport. In the 1830s hunters shot so many pigeons for shipment to Eastern restaurants that a few days' shooting filled entire railroad boxcars. By 1914 the passenger pigeon was declared extinct in the United States.

When the settlers reached the Great Plains, historians estimate that some fifty to sixty million bison and forty million pronghorn lived there. The bison were the first to go. They were killed by hunters for their hides and their meat—and to loosen the hold of the American Indian on his ancestral hunting grounds.

Livestock syndicates based in the East and in Europe annihilated bison by the millions and replaced them with cows. Grizzly bears that had followed the bison herds retreated to the mountains where they preyed on deer, elk, and lesser game.

Wolves and coyotes turned to the cattle and sheep herds that now grazed on the former bison lands; as a result they were labeled as "varmints" and shot. Ranchers poisoned untold millions of prairie dogs because the rodents dug burrows that could break the leg of a cow or a horse.

Now the railroads pushed west to meet trailheads for the cattle drives that were bringing livestock from the Plains to Eastern markets. As soon as the railroads were laid, travelers rode them out to the "Wild West" where part of the experience was to eat Western food such as venison and bison steaks. From 1870 to 1900 thousands of bison, elk, deer, pronghorn, and prairie chickens were killed by "market hunters" to satisfy the vacationers' taste for wild game.

Later, industrial plants, mines, hydroelectric ventures, and housing and shopping developments further transformed the landscape. Highways crisscrossed the continent. Airplanes opened remote wilderness areas to sportsmen.

By now many Americans realized that a number of species of animals had been wiped out and other species were in danger of eradication. The tide of public opinion began to turn from an acceptance of indiscriminate killing of animals for food and fur to the conservation of wildlife as a part of the nation's natural heritage.

In 1872 Congress set aside Yellowstone National Park as the first natural sanctuary in the country, for that matter in the world. The legislation not only preserved the unique geological features of Yellowstone, such as its thermal fields, but also preserved within its boundaries one of the last remaining bison herds. This group of thirty-nine animals has since served as the nucleus of several healthy herds that thrive in the United States today.

A number of states had already adopted—and enforced—game laws to limit the killing of wildlife. In 1890 Congress reinforced the state regulations. It passed the Lacey Act, which prohibited the interstate shipment of game taken in violation of state laws, effectively putting the large-scale "market hunters" out of business.

In 1891 Congress established the first forest preserve, reserving forested land that would produce a regulated supply of timber and provide habitat for wildlife. This forestland, first designated as the Yellowstone Park Timberland Reserve, continues as the Shoshone National Forest in Wyoming. In 1901 the U.S. Forest Service was authorized under the Department of Agriculture to oversee the growing number of national forests.

President Theodore Roosevelt in 1903 established the nation's first wildlife refuge, Pelican Island in Florida, to shield nesting birds from hunters. Other refuges, such as the Wichita Mountains National Wildlife Refuge and the National Bison Range in Montana, were set aside to protect mammals.

In 1916 Congress established the National Park Service within the Department of the Interior to protect the outstanding natural and cultural resources of the country, including the wild animals that live in them.

Other landmark legislation followed, including the Federal Aid in Wildlife Restoration (Pittman-Robertson) Act of 1918, which provided funds from federal excise taxes on hunting weapons to replenish populations of game animals.

In 1940 Congress organized the U.S. Fish and Wildlife Service under the Department of the Interior to supervise the wildlife refuges and to conserve both the nation's wildlife and its habitat.

In addition to these efforts within government, a number of private wildlife conservation organizations have been formed since the turn of the century, including the National Audubon Society, Isaak Walton League, Sierra Club, National Wildlife Federation, Wilderness Society, and Defenders of Wildlife.

Where Wildlife Roams Free

In spite of the settlement, cultivation, industrialization, and development of the United States, a surprising one-third of the nation's land remains in the public domain—either federal, state, county, or city. It is on these lands that you will likely find some of your best wildlife watching opportunities.

Let's take a closer look at some of these preserves.

National Wildlife Refuges

The 448 national wildlife refuges in the United States surpass those of any other nation in the diversity of their habitats and the number of wild creatures protected within them. No fewer than 220 species of mammals, 600 species of birds, 250 species of reptiles and amphibians, 200 species of fish, and uncounted kinds of insects and plants live in these refuges.

The U.S. Fish and Wildlife Service of the Department of the Interior is responsible for maintaining and protecting these wildlife resources. It manages migratory birds and endangered wildlife, preserving the habitat these animals need. Fish and Wildlife biologists carry out research on animals to foster healthy populations.

Many refuges were established to protect animal populations that were threatened. Pelican Island National Wildlife Refuge, for example, was authorized to shield brown pelicans, herons, and egrets from being needlessly slaughtered for their plumes, which were used in ladies' hats.

The Wichita Mountains Wildlife Refuge in Oklahoma and the National Bison Range in Montana were established to protect the bison. Kofa Game Range in Arizona and Desert National Wildlife Range in Nevada protect desert bighorn sheep. Charles Sheldon Antelope Range in Nevada and Hart Mountain National Antelope Refuge in Oregon sustain the pronghorn, while the National Elk Refuge in Wyoming protects elk.

Many refuges provide a sanctuary for birds while they are breeding, migrating, or wintering along the four major flyways that span the country from north to south. A number of these refuges and waterfowl production areas are located in the north-central part of the country where "prairie potholes" provide excellent breeding ground for birds.

Refuge biologists also are working to restore several endangered species of birds, such as the whooping crane, to healthy populations.

Remember, when you visit a refuge that the needs of the animals come first. Grass and shrubs are allowed to

Rarely will the shy mountain goat allow a person (such as the author's wife) to approach so closely. Mountain goats and a variety of other wild animals find suitable habitat at wilderness preserves like Glacier National Park in Montana.

grow high and go to seed to benefit the wildlife populations. Refuge managers actively seek to improve the
habitat by building impoundments to collect water, plant-
ing crops to provide forage, and using controlled burning
to improve feeding and nesting grounds for wildlife.

About two-thirds of the refuges are open to the public. Most have a visitor center for orientation and exhibits of local wildlife. It's best to begin your exploration
here, where staff members can acquaint you with their
mammal and bird lists and provide you with a map of the
refuge.

Many refuges have roads for auto touring and nature
trails for hiking, but they do not usually provide campgrounds, personally guided walks, or demonstrations.
Leaflets help you find significant habitats along the tour
routes and trails. A number of refuges have photo or
observation blinds that you can use.

Visitor centers are usually open from Monday
through Friday each week and closed on weekends. The
refuges themselves, however, are usually open every day.
Some stay open during spring, summer, and fall but close
during the winter.

National Forests

The Forest Service of the U.S. Department of Agriculture
manages its vast forests and grasslands largely for the
production of timber for wood and paper products.

In its 156 national forests and other lands it balances
timber production with other public benefits, including
natural beauty, wildlife habitat, wilderness, mineral production, water supply, and livestock forage. The hall-
mark of the national forests is "multiple use," whereby
each forest serves several purposes at the same time.

The national forests provide Americans more than
forty percent of all recreation pursued on federal public
land. Leisure activities range from swimming and boating on lakes and rivers to pleasure driving, from hiking
and camping to skiing and wildlife watching.

A few of the more popular national forests have a
visitor center where you will find displays, audio-visual
programs, and printed material that explain the forest
resources and activities.

If no visitor center exists, you should probably visit
the forest supervisor's office, located in a town near the
forest. Here you can get maps of the forest area, maps of
hiking trails that have good potential for seeing wildlife,
and perhaps a bird and mammal list. The office also may
have a selection of books that describe the area. If you
have specific questions about a certain species, ask to
talk with the wildlife management specialist on the staff.

As you drive the roads through the forest you may
pass a district ranger's office. Its employees and volunteers carry out the day-to-day operations of the forest,
such as managing timber sales, overseeing recreation
activities, and monitoring the wildlife that makes its

home in the forest. Feel free to drop in and ask about recent animal sightings, required permits, or the best roads on which to observe wildlife.

You may find another source of information at one of the many Forest Service campgrounds. The Service maintains some five thousand campgrounds as part of its multiple use management of the forest land.

At one of the larger campgrounds you may meet a campground host, often a retired person who volunteers to live at the campground during the visitor season, offer advice to campers, make sure the campground rules are followed, and respond in an emergency.

Your campground host knows the territory—and the animals in it. He will no doubt be glad to share his insights and give you tips on what to look for.

National Parks

National parks protect and maintain some of the most spectacular landscapes in America as well as many of the nation's most significant historic landmarks.

Of these, thirty-nine of the largest and most scenic areas are designated as "national parks." Other preserves among the 354 units of the national park system bear titles that reflect the nature of the resource: national historical park, national seashore, national river, national recreation area, national parkway, national memorial, national site.

The mission of the National Park Service of the Department of the Interior is to preserve these scenic wonders in their natural condition along with the plants and animals that live in them. At the same time, the Park Service encourages the public to view and enjoy this scenery, vegetation, and wildlife.

In carrying out its mission the Park Service generally lets nature take its course. Rangers do not haul away downed trees, replant seedlings after a fire, or bring sand to replace a washed-out beach. They explain that such events are manifestations of nature and that nature will in time heal the wounds.

On approaching a national park you may pick up an announcement on your radio describing the park, mentioning seasonal activities, and suggesting you begin at the visitor center. At the entrance gate a park ranger collects an entrance fee and gives you a park map and perhaps a park newspaper listing the activities offered.

The visitor center serves as your best information source and hub of park activities. The ranger behind the counter is ready to answer your questions or find someone who can.

The rangers are devoted to interpreting the park's resources. They inform the visitor in many ways: through campfire talks, guided hikes, nature walks, boat trips, wayside exhibits, demonstrations, films, children's programs, and a wide variety of printed material including mammal and bird lists and trail maps. Self-guiding folders explaining what you will see along a trail are often available for a modest fee at the trailhead.

Great Smoky Mountains National Park, for example, publishes a set of six folders on different aspects of the park. A folder entitled "Wildlife" summarizes the most common large and small mammals, birds, snakes, amphibians, lizards, and fish found in the park. At the Sugarlands Visitor Center is a notable collection of mounted wildlife specimens. Getting a close-up view of an animal makes it that much easier to later recognize the animal in its natural surroundings.

Each park hires seasonal rangers during peak visitor seasons to carry out its interpretive programs. The seasonals, all carefully selected, are often high school or college teachers who know their natural history. Take an orientation hike, attend a nature talk, or take your questions to these ranger-naturalists, and you'll quickly become acquainted with the park's animal life. A good seasonal ranger usually succeeds in transforming the visiting spectator into a participant.

When you arrive at a park or refuge, it is a good idea to stop first at the visitor center to get a mammal list, a trail map, and details of recent wildlife sightings. At Rocky Mountain National Park, Ranger Stephanie Chapman advises visitors Gregory and Elaine Sevener of Marinette, Wisconsin.

District rangers and campground hosts can also aid the wildlife observer. District rangers, who are responsible for the smooth operation of a section of the park, can help you with specific questions about animals common in their sector. Campground hosts have the same function as in national forests. Marge and I spent an entertaining hour one night prowling a campground in the Great Smoky Mountains looking for a raccoon our campground host said was a regular scavenger. We failed to spot the raccoon that night but we observed plenty of raccoon signs and made a new friend in our knowledgeable host.

Some of the larger national parks have comfortable lodges for overnight accommodations. Many ranger-led walks and talks originate at these lodges. If you're looking for even more information you may find a two- or three-day course in wildlife offered at one of some twenty institutes that are associated with the national parks (see appendix).

National parks are open every day of the year, except one or two holidays. During peak season, visitor centers normally are open from 8 A.M. until 6 P.M. The rest of the year their hours are 9 A.M. to 5 P.M.

Bureau of Land Management

The Bureau of Land Management of the Department of the Interior administers no less than 327 million acres of public lands—an area that exceeds that of all the states along the Atlantic seaboard.

On these lands, most of which are in the West or in Alaska, BLM follows the principles of multiple use. It leases land for livestock grazing, mining of minerals such as coal, oil and gas exploration and production, and timber harvesting. Other lands are devoted to wilderness, outdoor recreation, and fish and wildlife development.

BLM manages the diverse wildlife habitats on these lands, usually in partnership with the state where the lands lie. It seeks to improve the habitat by restoring lands that have been disturbed by mining, protecting endangered species of wildlife, and monitoring animal populations to see if they are increasing or decreasing.

These vast tracts offer animals room to roam. In the Whiskey Mountains of Wyoming, for example, the largest herd of Rocky Mountain bighorn sheep in the country spends each winter.

BLM also runs a wild horse program, rounding up many of the wild horses that roam the wide open spaces and selling them for a small fee to people who will "adopt" the animals and give them a good home.

The bureau also administers the Snake River Birds of Prey Natural Area in Idaho, a region of desert, river, and cliffs that provides an excellent nesting area for golden eagles, peregrine falcons, prairie falcons, and other raptors.

Under the slogan "Watchable Wildlife," BLM identifies promising sites for wildlife viewing. On some of its lands it provides roadside pull-offs and identifying signs that guide you to good wildlife-watching spots.

Military Installations

Base commanders of the armed forces, in addition to carrying out their mission of national defense, are required to protect the natural resources on their public lands, including the fish and wildlife. Many people are surprised to discover that a number of military bases around the country allow access to citizens who want to enjoy these natural resources through wildlife watching, bird watching, hiking, picnicking, nature photography, hunting, or fishing.

Regulations vary, depending upon the mission of the installation. Some bases enhance the habitat for fish and wildlife, providing outdoor recreation opportunities primarily for their own military personnel and their families. Other bases allow ready access to wildlife areas or use a permit system to admit hunters and fishermen.

Tyndall Air Force Base in Florida, for example, invites wildlife watchers to hike a 1.6-mile nature trail that circles a lake and offers an opportunity to see alligators, waterfowl, and pond life. The trail, as well as much of the base, is open to the public.

At Camp LeJeune Marine Corps Base in North Carolina the public is free to drive through forested backcountry to look for black bear, white-tailed deer, and wild turkeys.

At Barksdale Air Force Base in Louisiana visitors may use two nature trails, a family camping area, and two parks on the reservation. Like many bases, Barksdale provides cooperative outdoor experiences for Boy and Girl Scouts, university forestry and wildlife classes, high school science classes, and wildlife clubs.

Patuxent River Naval Air Test Center in Maryland maintains a public overlook on the base for viewing waterfowl. An environmental education center displays live and mounted animal specimens, an observation beehive, terrariums, and bird nest boxes that attract some two hundred visitors a week during the summer.

At the Air Force Academy in Colorado the public is welcome to hike a one-half-mile environmental trail through this eighteen-thousand-acre wildlife preserve. Most observers have no trouble sighting some of the twelve hundred mule deer that reside in the woods and occasionally even wander onto the concrete Academy parade grounds.

State Lands

States preserve wildlife within state parks, state forests, and state game lands. Altogether, state recreation lands add up to some ninety-six thousand square miles—an area larger than Great Britain.

State parks preserve land in its natural state and foster recreational activities such as swimming, boating, picnicking, camping, organized sports, and hiking. A number of state parks preserve a variety of animals within their boundaries and many have nature programs and exhibits to acquaint visitors with them.

Custer State Park in South Dakota is exceptional; it boasts one of the largest publicly owned bison herds in the country and an eighteen-mile Wildlife Loop Road that guides the visitor who wants to see bison as well as elk, mule deer, white-tailed deer, pronghorn, and coyotes.

Brazos Bend State Park, thirty miles southwest of Houston, Texas, provides fifteen miles of trails and boardwalks over marshy terrain. A trail walk gives you a good look at a variety of wading birds, alligators, and white-tailed deer.

Prairie State Park, thirty miles north of Joplin, Missouri, preserves twenty-three species, including bison, prairie chicken, opossum, coyote, bobcat, ground squirrel, and skunk. It also protects a section of original tallgrass prairie that has never been cultivated.

In California, Anza-Borrego Desert State Park, just east of San Diego, protects four hundred desert bighorn sheep in its sandy washes and desert buttes. The park's visitor center is built underground to keep visitors cool in the hot desert climate.

Although the main mission of state forests is to manage timberlands to produce lumber, many of these lands hold populations of wildlife as well.

At Stillwater State Forest in northwestern Montana, for example, deer, black and grizzly bear, elk, moose, beaver, and marten all roam the woods. Wildlife watching is permitted, as is seasonal hunting and trapping.

States that manage lands as fish and game preserves do so primarily for the benefit of fishermen and hunters, although some assist wildlife observers by providing self-guiding trails, exhibits, and an occasional nature center. In Michigan the state has built several observation towers and walking trails so that wildlife watchers can get a good view of the flocks of migrating waterfowl flying north over the Great Lakes each spring.

Public Utilities

When it issues a license for the construction or renewal of a hydroelectric power project, the federal government requires that a power company improve or develop the waterway in ways that will benefit the public.

In response to this requirement, a number of electric power companies across the country have developed recreational facilities on their lands, which are often extensive. In Pennsylvania, for example, power companies are the second largest landowner behind the state itself. The facilities they offer range from swimming to camping to ice skating and may include wildlife observation.

At its pumped-storage generating facility and reservoirs near Northfield, Massachusetts, Northeast Utilities provides twenty-five miles of hiking and nature study trails, picnic areas, two campgrounds, canoeing, boating, fishing, and a recreation and environmental education center. A riverboat takes people on cruises along a twelve-mile section of the Connecticut River. Viewing windows at a fishway allow visitors to watch shad and salmon swim upriver past the dam.

On the lower Susquehanna River, the Philadelphia Electric Company generates electricity at the Conowingo Dam, which spans the river, at its Muddy Run pumped-storage reservoir, and at its Peach Bottom nuclear power plant. It offers recreational opportunities on the lands surrounding the complex. Some four hundred deer roam the woods and fields. Small mammals include rabbits, woodchucks, raccoons, foxes, and skunks. An increasing number of bald eagles come to catch fish in the turbulent water of the Conowingo Dam (see pages 74–75).

To help families and students from nearby schools enjoy wildlife, the company operates a busy environmental center. Staff instructors give workshops, nature walks, talks, and slide programs. Mounted animal specimens and graphic displays portray the wildlife that awaits outside.

"We can almost promise that if you walk the trails here you will see a deer," said David Ellenberg, manager of the Muddy Run Recreation Park.

He pointed out that power companies like Philadelphia Electric maintain miles of transmission lines that cross the countryside on rights-of-way up to 150 feet wide. These rights-of-way not only provide an avenue to carry electricity to the consumer but also furnish a natural habitat for mammals and birds. The company cuts the vegetation from time to time to keep growth down; as a result the shrubs, berry bushes, and high grass provide miles of meadow and brush that offer excellent food sources to a wide variety of animals.

To find out what your local power company offers in wildlife habitat, simply call or write the company's main office. Organizations are usually happy to share their recreational facilities.

Business and Industry

Other corporations are looking over their landholdings with an eye toward habitat for wildlife. Timber companies, whose holdings often encompass thousands of acres of forestland, sometimes provide campgrounds and facilities for wildlife watching.

A number of corporations have joined with conservation organizations in a Wildlife Habitat Enhancement Council to look for ways to put undeveloped corporate lands to use for the benefit of populations of animals, fish, and plants.

The DuPont Company has reintroduced ospreys to an island it owns in the Ohio River near Parkersburg, West Virginia. If the project is successful, bird watchers along the river will be able to watch these fast-diving birds plunge to the water's surface to grasp a fish in their talons.

At a plant operated by Remington Arms in Arkansas employees did much of the work, while the company provided equipment and financial support, to clear tall brush to provide browse and cover for deer and bob-white quail. They also planted grain as food for wild turkeys.

On 150 acres surrounding a medical systems manu-facturing plant in Wisconsin, General Electric planted grasses and wildflowers to restore a patch of former prairie. Volunteers also dug a pond and planted corn to attract migratory waterfowl, a project that demonstrated that not only government agencies but also business and industry can play a constructive role in preserving wild-life.

How Rangers Reveal
the World of Wildlife

Clare Landry, a veteran seasonal ranger at Glacier National Park, led us over to the counter at the St. Mary Visitor Center. Flipping open a black looseleaf notebook that bore the title "Wildlife Observation Report," he ran his finger down a column of entries: "Mountain goat, coyote, great blue heron, bighorn sheep, golden eagle, moose. . . ."

"These are the animal sightings our visitors have passed along to us the last two weeks," he said. "We encourage them to report sightings. It helps us to help other visitors."

Clare explained that rangers who patrol the park report the animals they see, as well as road kills, and that the staff also collects sighting information passed along by visitors—hence the black notebook. These sightings helped us find the wildlife we sought on our visit.

This is an example of the helpful guidance you will receive as you explore our national parks and forests, wildlife refuges, and state parks. By checking in at a visitor center as soon as you arrive, you can get a head start, thanks to the help of those who know the area best.

Many parks publish a newspaper during the visitor season that lists ranger talks, walks, excursions, self-guided trails, and demonstrations available to visitors. You will probably find, as we did, that these ranger-guided activities are a great help in locating and appreciating the wildlife you want to see.

Ranger Talks

One of the techniques long used by National Park Service rangers to impart information to visitors is the "campfire talk" or "ranger talk." In the early days these talks were usually presented to a group of visitors as they sat around a campfire.

Now many of the talks are given during the day at or near a visitor center where park visitors normally congregate. Some rangers give talks at the overnight lodges. In the evening a ranger usually speaks at an amphitheater located within a campground—either with or without the glow of the traditional campfire.

One August evening we joined a hundred other visitors in the auditorium of the Mammoth Hot Springs Hotel in Yellowstone National Park to hear a ranger discuss the park's endangered species, animals we hoped to see during our four-day visit.

Yellowstone protects four endangered species, Seasonal Ranger Janet Ellis told us: the grizzly bear, whooping crane, peregrine falcon, and bald eagle.

In the 1960s and 1970s Yellowstone Park enforced a bear management plan to save the grizzlies. It encouraged bears to forage for food on their own in the backcountry rather than take handouts of human food as they had in earlier years. The plan eliminated waste dumps where bears had been feeding, convinced campers to keep their food out of reach of animals, and dissuaded visitors from feeding bears that appear along roads. As a result the bear population in Yellowstone is truly wild again, existing as part of the Greater Yellowstone Ecosystem.

"They're out in the backcountry being bears," said Janet. " Sure, they're harder to see now, but if you do see one, think what a thrill it will be!"

Our speaker also noted that the National Park Service wants to reintroduce yet another endangered species to Yellowstone: the gray wolf. The wolves would join the grizzlies and black bears, mountain lions, wolverines, bobcats, coyotes, and foxes as predators in Yellowstone. These predators help maintain nature's balance among the tens of thousands of elk; thousands of bison and mule deer; hundreds of bighorn sheep, pronghorns, and moose; and uncounted rabbits and rodents.

We recalled Janet's talk on another day at Shenandoah National Park in Virginia where we heard a ranger talk on another endangered species: the peregrine falcon. Ranger Rick Potvin was discussing birds of prey.

Rick not only spoke about these unique birds, he showed them to us. From cages in the rear of his van he produced a red-tailed hawk, a barred owl, and a peregrine falcon. All three of the birds had been injured and would not have survived had they been returned to the wild.

Asking questions of his audience, he extracted from us three important characteristics of a bird of prey. We agreed that a bird of prey needed to have strong talons to grab its prey, a sharp beak to tear into flesh, and excellent eyesight to spy its quarry from high in the sky. All birds of prey also must be masters of flight.

After a ranger talk, Ranger Bill Christianson tells visitors Jeff Kuzinic and his son how to distinguish an elk's large antlers (left) from a mule deer's smaller ones. Both of these hoofed mammals lose their antlers each year, then grow new ones.

He pointed out that birds of prey do much to keep the rodent population under control. "A wood rat will eat the eggs laid by a grouse, but a bird of prey may hunt and kill the rat. As a result other grouse eggs will escape the rat's appetite, the remaining grouse eggs will hatch, and the grouse will continue to exist as a species."

He carefully eased the falcon from its cage and coaxed it to stand on his gloved wrist. Keeping a leather tether firmly attached to one of the bird's feet, Rick deftly removed a hood from its head. The bird flapped its powerful wings as if to take off. Rick inverted his wrist, the wings stopped beating, and soon the falcon was standing upright once more, perched quietly atop Rick's wrist.

Perhaps the fastest bird in the sky, the peregrine can dive at up to 175 miles an hour. With great speed it hits a slow flying bird (such as a duck) with its feet, knocking it senseless. The falcon then dives again and collects its prey after it falls to the ground.

Rick concluded by relating the success story of the peregrine falcon. When the pesticide DDT came into wide use in the 1960s, the number of peregrines mysteriously diminished. Eventually biologists discovered that female falcons that had ingested DDT laid eggs with thin shells too fragile to hatch. Since the use of DDT was prohibited in 1972, the swiftest bird in the air is making a strong comeback.

Ranger Walks

A walk with a ranger can add a new dimension to your wildlife observation: you are now entering the animal's habitat. What's more, you have a trained observer at your side who knows the territory.

Fifteen of us gathered at a bridge over McDonald Creek in Glacier National Park early one afternoon to take a 2½-mile hike with Seasonal Ranger Jan Anthony. Jan told us she had worked for several years at an archaeological dig at Chaco Canyon, New Mexico, for part of each year, and had returned to Glacier each summer.

On this hike through a mature forest of lodgepole pine, Jan informed us we would see a beautiful waterfall where the creek cascaded over rocks—and if we were lucky, we might spot a moose.

Like most interpretive rangers, Jan had a theme for our walk. She compared the structure of the forest to the organization of a city.

The leafy tops of the trees, she explained, were like the penthouses of tall city buildings, home to the birds. The trunks represented the offices of a skyscraper. The tenants include woodpeckers busy drilling for grubs and squirrels running up and down on numerous errands.

At the base of the tree, analogous to the ground level of a skyscraper, traffic swirls. Mice, chipmunks, and ground squirrels make their homes under logs. Small mammals such as foxes, raccoons, and bobcats wander by, stopping to forage for fast food.

A tree's root system represents the basement of the building. Here is located the machinery that makes the building run—the lifegiving roots of the tree, soil, and water. Below ground live the "engineers" of the animal world, the burrowing creatures like mice, shrews, voles, and moles.

As we continued single file up the trail, one of the young girls in our group heard a branch crack and noticed movement to her left. We passed her whispered alert up the line and Jan quickly brought us to a halt.

We all peered through the dimness. Past crowded tree trunks we could make out a large animal with a shiny, dark brown coat moving slowly, grazing.

"It's a cow moose," Jan announced as a battery of binoculars were raised into position like deck guns on a cruiser. As we watched, the moose's brown flanks disappeared into the dark depths of the forest.

Our young friend was the heroine of the afternoon for spotting the moose. For most of us it was our first glimpse, however fleeting, of this dignified denizen of the wilderness.

How much natural history education you can pack into a ranger walk was illustrated for us when we took a twilight walk at Grand Teton National Park in Wyoming with Seasonal Ranger Sheila Willis. Before coming to Teton, Sheila, a native Georgian, had served as a sea-

Rangers know the territory and can often improve your chances of seeing wild animals. Adults and children listen as Ranger Sarah Webb at Shenandoah National Park explains the habits of the white-tailed deer they hope to see.

sonal at Okefenokee National Wildlife Refuge in Georgia, Great Smoky Mountains National Park in Tennessee, and Yellowstone National Park in Wyoming; so she knew her way around the woods. She guided our group of twenty campers and visitors on a three-mile walk that proved to be a bonanza of wildlife signs and animal sightings.

First we got an accelerated course in "reading" wildlife signs. Sheila pointed out scratches on a pine tree where a black bear had climbed eight feet up the trunk, then scrambled down again. Smooth rub marks on another tree trunk were a tip-off that a mule deer had scratched its antlers against the bark to ease the itching of the velvet. Sheila added that when the male mule deer finally sheds its antlers, the bones are gradually consumed by mice and other rodents who need the nutrients.

Deep, rectangular gouge marks scarred another tree trunk. A porcupine at work, Sheila said. For winter sustenance, the porcupine chews these rectangular scars into a tree trunk to get down to the succulent cambian layer. Sometimes the animal gnaws completely around the trunk, causing the girdled tree to die.

"Porcupines are active at night," she said. "They sleep during the day high in a tree where you're not likely to see them. They blend so well with their surroundings it has taken me almost the whole summer to finally see one."

Every turn in the trail seemed to reveal another sign: a rotting log torn apart by a bear searching for grubs, a badger's burrow, coyote scat (droppings) that contained evidence of fur remaining from the coyote's last meal.

We came across the browse line on several trees where a moose had gnawed during the winter.

"Did the moose have a park permit to do that?" joked one of our group.

"He didn't need a permit," Sheila responded. "It's his park!"

As we neared a small lake we saw the animals themselves. A flock of Canada geese flew overhead, preparing to head south on this late August day. Two elegant trumpeter swans, their graceful white bodies accented by black beaks, patrolled the lake. A V-shaped break in the smooth surface of the water was a muskrat heading home with some twigs in its mouth.

Sheila suggested we focus our binoculars on the grassy island not far from the shore. Sure enough, something rustled in the grass. Eventually the head of a cow moose, then a calf, appeared. Moose, we learned, feed on willows and bottom-rooted aquatic plants in the summer, then revert to tree bark and twigs of fir, willow, birch, and aspen in the winter.

The finale of the evening's wildlife show came when we reached a beaver lodge. Marge and I had seen several beaver dams and lodges before but had never discovered one with active beavers.

Tonight was different. On the shore near the lodge two beavers were hard at work. One swam gracefully to the bank, climbed out of the water, and awkwardly waddled up the slope. Grasping a mouthful of vegetation, it waddled back to the water, slid into a canal it had built into the bank, and swam back to its lodge, disappearing under the surface to find its underwater entrance.

The beavers were working so hard, Sheila said, because they had to build a new lodge before winter set in. Their former lodge was no longer safe from predators because the summer drought had drained away most of the water surrounding it. The entrance was now vulnerable because it was above water rather than below it.

The beavers' bad luck was our good fortune. Since the animals had to go back into the construction business, it gave us a great opportunity to watch these environmental engineers of the backcountry.

Ranger walks can set you on the high road to adventure as well as give you new insights into the world of animals. Marge and I had a rendezvous with adventure—and mountain goats—on another hike at Glacier, the mile-high Highline Trail.

Our ranger-guide was Mike Wacker, a sturdily built outdoorsman and a member of the Blackfeet Indian tribe. Mike was working as a ranger for the summer, and then planned to return to the University of Wisconsin to complete his bachelor's degree in geology.

Our mission for today was to follow Mike three miles along a narrow alpine trail, along rocky ledges and across tumbling streams to Haystack Butte where, he said, there was a good chance we'd see mountain goats.

The trail begins near the Logan Pass Visitor Center (elevation 6,684 feet), which sits atop the Continental Divide. Snow still lay cradled in the upper reaches of the mountains. Part of the trail parallels the Going-to-the-Sun Road, the cross-park road completed in 1933 in an epic civil engineering achievement.

As our group of eighteen started out, Mike counseled everyone about places where the narrow trail skirted precipitous drops down the mountainside. "Look at your feet, not the scenery," he warned. He explained that trail etiquette requires hikers to walk single file so that oncoming hikers can pass. When we stopped occasionally to catch our breath, he described the alpine flowers, the mountain formations, and the changes wrought by avalanches and fires.

At one point Mike held his hand up for everyone to stop and remain quiet. A hoary marmot, gray in front and brown toward the rear, stood like a tiny sentinel on a rock, then skittered away, emitting a shrill whistle to warn other marmots of the intruders. The marmot, also called a rockchuck, is one of the largest ground squirrels. It can grow to two feet in length and may weigh up to twelve pounds.

We also saw one of the marmot's smaller relatives, the Columbian ground squirrel. These little rodents run in fast zigzags as they race about to find seeds and nuts, then dive between rocks to hide from predators like hawks.

After a 1½-hour hike we came to the foot of Haystack Butte. Mike led us across a jumble of rocks to an open sweep of mountainside cut by a steep rock cliff.

He scanned the rock face with his binoculars. Nothing in sight. He looked again, sweeping his binoculars across the rocks.

"There they are," he announced triumphantly. Binoculars were whipped out of trail packs as everyone focused on Mike's find.

Five mountain goats stepped carefully in single file along a high ledge on the cliff face. Mike identified the leader as a ram, followed by two nannies and two kids.

Like all kids the two little goats jumped across crevices that the adults walked around. Down the terraced slope they came, now moving in one direction, now switching back the other way, coming ever closer to the point where we stood.

Mike relaxed against a rock, decreeing a lunch break. But everyone else watched the goats. Binoculars and cameras with telephoto lenses followed the white forms down the rocks.

"Do they know we're here?" a girl asked. Mike said he was sure they did because goats have superb eyesight.

Someone else asked how they kept their balance. Mike described what he called their "Velcro pads," the soft surfaces that mountain goats have on the underpart of each hoof.

"What do they find to eat up there?" wondered another in our group. Lichens, leaves, grass, and small bushes and berries, Mike answered.

After half an hour the goats had descended to a patch of green grass two hundred yards upslope from where we stood. Reluctantly we left when Mike said it

An elk's jaw and teeth enable it to grind up and swallow the twigs, bark, and tree buds that make up a large part of its diet. Rangèr Jean Muenchrath holds the jawbone for observation by visitors to Rocky Mountain National Park.

was time to return to Logan Pass. We reached our destination in late afternoon, just in time to get a lesson in the wrong way for people to treat mountain goats.

From our vantage point on the trail above the Going-to-the-Sun Road we could see a young billy goat standing in a crowded turnout. Traffic was backing up as cars pulled into the turnout and passengers jumped out, leaving doors ajar, to photograph the goat or tempt it with food. The people on foot, the passing motorists, and the goat were all being put at risk.

Mike pulled his walkie-talkie from his belt and radioed the visitor center for a ranger to chase the goat away to avoid a dangerous traffic snarl. Then he explained why feeding wild animals is a disservice to them. It was the first of many examples on our trip of one of the most persistent problems faced by park and refuge managers: how to convince visitors that feeding wild animals tampers with nature's balance, harms the animals and is a risk for visitors (see page 152).

Special Excursions

At a few national parks and wildlife refuges visitors are offered innovative excursions to give them a closer look at the native animals.

At Aransas National Wildlife Refuge in Texas a cabin cruiser takes boatloads of visitors through refuge waterways to view the rare whooping crane and other shore and wading birds.

At the privately operated Jackson Hole Ski Resort near Grand Teton National Park, you may ride a tramway to the top of 10,783-foot Rendezvous Peak. Here a staff naturalist employed by the resort helps you observe the pikas and marmots that inhabit this rocky, windswept mountaintop.

At Shark Valley in the northern part of Everglades National Park in Florida an open-sided tram takes wildlife watchers along a fifteen-mile roadway built above the watery terrain. From the tram you get a good view across this vast wet plain, the largest subtropical wilderness in the United States. You see alligators only a few feet away basking in the sun or slithering into a slough.

At the end of the elevated roadway stands a spiral-shaped observation tower. From atop the tower you look down on alligators, turtles, and wading birds that use the waterhole beneath you. A ranger is on hand to allay the fears of some visitors and to reveal interesting facts about the alligator, an animal that once was endangered but in recent years has made a strong comeback.

A popular way to see wildlife at Great Smoky Mountains National Park is to hop aboard a hayride that circles the Cades Cove valley. The Cades Cove riding stable offers the ride several times a day, often accompanied by a park ranger.

"Families like the hayride," Seasonal Ranger Michele Maertens told us. "The kids love it and so do their parents. And it gives us rangers a chance to talk to a lot of people at the same time."

We joined a hundred other people the October evening when Marge and I took the ride. Farm trucks pulled two hay-filled wagons on the eleven-mile tour through pasture, thick forests, and pioneer homesteads. We stopped several times as Michele pointed out white-tailed deer grazing in a meadow and woodchucks standing tall in a field. In vain we peered into forests trying to spot a black bear.

At one stop Michele held up several photographs. This, she said, is another wild animal that inhabits the Smokies—the wild hog. The hog is not native to the region; it was introduced years ago by sportsmen for hunting and has multiplied ever since.

Hogs root up and destroy wildflowers and plants with their snouts and sharp tusks. They destroy the eggs and offspring of turkeys and grouse; kill rabbits, fawns, and salamanders; compete with bears, deer, and squirrels for protein-rich acorns; and churn up mountain streams with their wallowing.

The growth of the hog population poses a serious problem for the park. Their rooting tears up the ground, killing vegetation and reducing good habitat for other animals. The Park Service is attempting to control their numbers through trapping and shooting.

The hay wagons returned after two hours with a laughing load of satisfied customers. Many riders described the hayride as the highlight of their park visit and a grand way to see wild animals in their own habitats without disturbing them.

Wayside Exhibits

Wayside exhibits—illustrated signs along a park road or trail—are another method used by rangers to provide wildlife watchers and other visitors with information. Wayside signs call attention to points of interest or describe natural or historic features. Other signs caution visitors against actions that might hurt themselves or the resource.

Even a cautionary sign can be educational. A rustic sign at Wind Cave National Park is entitled "Save This Prairie Dog Town." It warns visitors not to walk out onto the prairie dog settlement, thereby trampling the grass and forbs (any herb that is not grasslike) the rodents eat. "Artificial feeding," it continues, "compounds the problem with a poor diet," adding that visitors should not give human food to the animals.

We came upon another informative wayside exhibit at a parking area and trailhead at Shenandoah National Park in Virginia. An illustration under a roofed shelter informs the visitor that not all of Shenandoah's animals are easy to see. For example, it cautions, the deer mouse, red-backed salamander, and wood frog inhabit "small worlds" and are easily overlooked. The visitor is more likely to see "roadside visitors" like the white-tailed deer, opossum, ruffed grouse, and woodchuck. Finally, "wilderness residents" such as the black bear, wild turkey, and bobcat either stay far away from traveled routes or forage at night when they're less likely to be seen.

Another Shenandoah exhibit at a roadside overlook directs the visitor to take note of the area of brown, leafless forest on a facing hillside. The brown area, a contrast with the healthy green forest surrounding it, is the result of the work of the gypsy moth, the sign tells you.

In early summer, we learned, gypsy moth caterpillars feed on a variety of forest trees, with oak trees their favorite. In some areas they strip the forest bare. Many of the stripped trees, weakened by the gypsy moth attack, eventually die. Over time the forest replaces oaks with other trees less vulnerable to the gypsy moth.

The text concluded by pointing out that the forest had suffered other such changes, such as the chestnut blight of the 1920s and 1930s. Though changed, it said, Shenandoah's forest survived the blight, just as it will survive the gypsy moth.

Self-guided Tours

National parks, forests, and wildlife refuges cannot, of course, provide a ranger to interpret every trail. Thus, these public preserves have developed self-guided trails—some for walkers, others for autos.

A folder called a trail guide substitutes for the ranger on these do-it-yourself trails. The information in the trail guide is usually keyed to numbered markers along the path.

Self-guided footpaths are often loop trails that originate near a visitor center. Other self-guided trails begin at a turnout from a park road or from a parking area.

Auto tour roads circle through a park or refuge, leading past turnouts, scenic overlooks, and wayside exhibits. Self-guiding folders or tape cassettes providing narrations of interest points are often available.

Great Smoky Mountains National Park has a wide variety of both self-guided foot and auto trails. Locations of these trails are shown on the park map available at visitor centers.

The guide to one of these trails, the Balsam Mountain Trail, captures the visitor's interest right away: "Warning! The use of this trail could be habit-forming and beneficial to your health. Symptoms include heightened sensory awareness, intellectual refreshment and physical invigoration. . . . This forest is not marred with clocks. It is open, friendly, intimate and willing to display its valuables to those who wish to see them."

The guide for another trail, the Sugarlands Self-guiding Nature Trail, relates how deer and bear populations diminished as farmers settled in the mountain hollows, but increased again under the protection of the national park.

The narrative emphasizes patience. "If you sit on this hillside some evening," the folder says, "you might see deer, fox, bobcat or even bear or wild hog. But these animals mostly stay hidden. Smaller wildlife such as squirrels, chipmunks and many kinds of birds are much more common and more easily seen."

Rangers at Rocky Mountain National Park have marked the thirty-two stops on the Bear Lake Nature Trail with numbers outlined by bear prints. Chipmunks and ground squirrels greeted us the day we walked the half mile around the lake, guided by the attractive folder.

The Taggart Lake Trail in Grand Teton National Park tells a different story—the recovery of plants and wildlife after a fire in 1985 ravaged part of this lodgepole pine forest. Today the blackened logs are cloaked with new flowers and bushes and new saplings are sprouting. In a lodgepole forest, we learned, fire plays an important role. The intense heat of a fire causes lodgepole pine cones to open, discharging their seeds and regenerating the forest.

Now birds have returned. Deer browse in the new growth. New populations of insects and animals take up residence.

Even self-guided trails to historic sites offer wildlife lessons. The best group of badger holes we saw anywhere was at the historic Pierce Cunningham cabin at Grand Teton. Badger diggings dotted the sandy soil around the cabin. Our self-guiding folder told us why. Plenty of Uinta ground squirrels inhabit the grounds. For the badgers, the combination of plentiful prey and loose soil, which is easy to dig, makes for a happy hunting ground.

Arizona's Saguaro National Monument offers two auto tour roads and a number of side trails that teach lessons of the desert. To best see wildlife at a desert park, go out on the tour road in the early morning or close to dusk, advised Bob Hall, Saguaro's Chief of Resource Management.

So, in the early evening of a September day we took the six-mile tour road through a brown landscape dotted with huge saguaro cactuses and creosote bushes in the western part of the park. Our scorecard for an hour's slow drive included a jackrabbit, a desert tortoise, and a kit fox (a real triumph: the park ranger on duty said he hadn't seen one all summer). The fox ran across the road in front of our motor home, bushy tail held high, and disappeared in the brush on the other side.

We picked up some useful tips about watching wild-life from a motorized vehicle the day we toured the National Bison Range at Moiese, Montana, eighty miles south of Glacier National Park. The bison range, established in 1908, preserves one of the country's remaining herds of bison on nineteen thousand acres of grassland along the Flathead River.

We started off on the right foot by getting an early morning start (the refuge opens at 7 A.M.) and stopped first at the visitor center. Here we studied exhibits that tell the story of the tragic decimation of millions of bison that once roamed the prairies and of the efforts of a handful of conservationists to save the last few bison on preserves such as the National Bison Range.

At the information desk a clerk provided us with tips and a map of the nine-mile tour. We were told, first of all, to drive slowly. The refuge is home to not only some 350 to 450 bison but also 130 elk, 200 mule deer, 200 white-tailed deer, 40 bighorn sheep, 50 goats, and 150 pronghorns—not to mention badgers, mink, beavers, muskrats, weasels, bobcats, and coyotes.

Plan to stop frequently at turnoffs, the clerk advised, and use your binoculars to scan the rolling brown hills and low valleys. And don't forget to look back at the terrain you've just passed.

To spot a pronghorn, look for a splash of white against the brown hills—the pronghorn's distinctive white flanks and rump patch. Look for deer as they browse where trees and underbrush meet the open prairie.

Stay in your car and drive only on designated roads. Your vehicle serves as a good blind, allowing you to get closer to the animals than you might be able to on foot.

It's also safer to stay in your car. Wild animals are unpredictable. It is especially risky to get between a mother and her offspring. Leaving your car can also scare wildlife away from the road, taking away from the next visitor the pleasure of seeing these animals.

Anxious to see some wildlife and put this good advice into action, I climbed aboard our recreational vehicle, "Tortuga." The Spanish word for "turtle" seems appropriate for a vehicle that we use for wildlife adventure and that carries its home on its back. I propelled Tortuga up the twisting roadway at about twenty miles an hour as Marge swept the hills with her binoculars.

At Stop No. 2 on the self-guiding tour we parked at a turnout to walk a trail to an overlook. That's when we met Jerry Weslin, a store owner from Missoula, Montana. We never hesitated to talk to other visitors while looking for wild animals. We always felt that several pairs of eyes were better than two—other people may have seen animals we had not.

Since he and his family had been in the car just ahead of ours on this first lap of the tour, I asked him which animals they had seen so far. He surprised me by saying they had seen sixty to seventy bison, two elk, and a group of pronghorn.

When I told him we had seen only two bison, he smiled and said, "I told my wife I thought you were going too fast. Slow down a bit. Even stop once in a while and look around. The first time I came out here I drove too fast and didn't see a darned thing."

That taught us a lesson. We slowed down to five or ten miles an hour and stopped frequently. As a result we saw many more bison, a white-tailed buck, some twenty pronghorn and—to our great surprise—three bighorn rams. We were alerted to the bighorns by the couple in a car ahead of us who had pulled to the side of the road and signaled us to stop.

At another location Marge spotted a cloud of dust. Bringing the scene into focus, she discovered a cow bison taking a dust bath, a roll in the dirt that covers its coat with dust to ward off stinging flies.

From what Jerry and rangers at other parks have told us, we have found that remaining in your car, van, or recreational vehicle is an excellent strategy. Your car disguises your human smell, which animals quickly sense. They are accustomed to the smell of cars on a tour road. But as soon as you get out of your car, they pick up your scent and may move quickly away.

Animals are also keenly aware of noise. On a preserve like the National Bison Range they have learned to associate certain noises with human events. Keep your car running and the animal may pay no attention to you. Shutting the engine off may signal to the animal a threatening change, such as people getting out of their cars.

These wildlife tips proved worthwhile at the end of our afternoon at the bison range. As we slowly proceeded, some twenty pronghorns moved nonchalantly from one side of the road to the other, trotting across the road a few short feet in front of our vehicle while we admired them from our motorized blind.

Timely advice from people at a visitor center will make your wildlife watching more meaningful. Their in-depth training and first-hand knowledge can maximize your viewing opportunities. From the first ranger at the entrance gate and visitor's center to those who inform and lead you on talks, walks, and special excursions, all will help open doors to new knowledge.

Wildlife Education Programs

Yet another way to expand your wildlife knowledge is through an appealing selection of courses, seminars, workshops, and field trips offered by institutes associated with national parks and by other wildlife education organizations.

Courses range from a one-day field trip to a full semester's work that earns you credit at a sponsoring university. In between are two- or three-day short courses, family weekend outings, backcountry hiking and canoeing adventures, and photography and art workshops.

Most are taught by college or high school teachers who are authorities in their specialties and who enjoy teaching in an outdoor classroom. All classes are designed to teach you more than you can absorb through your car window and to offer some close-to-nature experiences.

"A number of people who come to Glacier National Park include one of our courses as part of their visit," said Ursula Mattson, director of the Glacier Institute, as she showed us the institute catalog. We could easily see why people would be attracted to course titles such as *Glacier's Grizzlies, Return of the Wolf,* and *Wildlife Tracking.*

At Yosemite National Park in California the emphasis is on in-depth study combined with rugged field observa-

The Versatile Ranger

As you visit national parks, wildlife refuges, and forests you will cross paths with a number of the professionals whose job it is to conserve these natural areas.

Duties and job titles vary, reflecting the differing missions of the National Park Service, the U.S. Fish and Wildlife Service, and the U.S. Forest Service. Park Service employees are known as rangers; in the Fish and Wildlife Service they are biologists, refuge managers, outdoor recreation planners, and park technicians; in the Forest Service they are mostly foresters or forest technicians. Beyond the job titles, there are several distinctions among these natural resource professionals wearing the uniforms and insignia of their individual agencies.

In the National Park Service, a ranger may be trained as a resource management ranger, an interpretive ranger, or a law enforcement ranger. Such specialties reflect the Park Service mission of preserving 354 outstanding natural and man-made landmarks and interpreting their scenic values and historic significance for the public. At every national park, interpretive rangers organize a variety of activities, including educational walks, talks, boat rides, and canoe trips to give visitors an understanding of the park and its resources. Exhibits, films, and displays add to the visitor's knowledge.

Other rangers, skilled in conservation, manage the natural resources of the park. Law enforcement rangers are trained to control the large number of people who enjoy the parks every year. Seasonal rangers—the rangers you typically see at entrance stations, campgrounds, and visitor center information desks—work for the Park Service during the peak visitor season.

Within the Fish and Wildlife Service, 448 national wildlife refuges and 28 wetland management districts conserve, protect, and enhance fish and wildlife and

tion. A three-day summer seminar, *Return of the Bighorn*, is limited to ten "hardy participants" who camp out overnight and scramble over rocks at ten thousand feet elevation as their instructors point out characteristics of the mountain sheep.

Most courses are not so strenuous. The popular Yellowstone Institute invites visitors to linger and learn at its rustic "Buffalo Ranch," once the center of the bison recovery program. The institute's twelve-page catalog tempts the traveler with one- to eight-day courses like *Mammal Tracking: Interpreting Tracks, Scat and Other Sign*, and *Yellowstone Bears, Folklore and Biology*. Participants stay in rustic cabins, which overlook the Lamar Valley, a haven for bison, elk, pronghorn, and mule deer.

Older Americans who want to enhance their understanding of wildlife can participate in Elderhostel, a nationwide educational program for older adults. A number of wildlife courses are among the thousands of classes offered to Elderhostel members each year at colleges and universities in all fifty states.

By requesting a copy of the Elderhostel catalog and planning ahead for your next wildlife-watching trip, you could enroll in a one-week course and later put your new

their habitats for the continuing benefit of Americans. Professional staffs at the refuges manage the populations of birds, animals, and fish that live in these preserves.

Most of the refuges are open to the public for wildlife-related activities such as wildlife observation, photography, hiking, fishing, and hunting—but not for camping or other recreation. Most refuges have a visitor center or contact station where a staff member or volunteer provides information. Refuges also provide self-guiding tour roads and nature trails, as well as observation towers for viewing migratory birds, fish, and mammals. Staff members often carry out environmental education study programs with schools and universities.

Refuge managers and their staffs monitor wildlife populations, improve habitat, encourage wildlife propagation, carry out research to protect the species, and enforce refuge regulations.

While protection of wildlife is the primary objective of the wildlife refuges, it is but one dimension of the Forest Service's mission. The foresters, biologists, and range conservationists of the Forest Service manage timber sales, maintain watersheds that provide water for nearby towns and cities, and supervise grazing lands for livestock, as well as protect the wildlife in the 156 national forests, 19 national grasslands, 13 national recreation areas, 21 national game refuges, and other areas administered by the Forest Service.

National forests also offer extensive recreation facilities: swimming, boating, fishing, pleasure driving, hiking, off-road vehicle driving, horseback riding, skiing, snowmobiling, wildlife watching, hunting, and camping. Where recreation facilities have been developed, interpretive specialists often guide walks and give talks at visitor centers and campgrounds. Maps of the forest roads and trails and perhaps a wildlife list are available at the visitor center, the forest supervisor's office, or district ranger's office.

knowledge into practice. At the University of Minnesota at Duluth one summer, for example, you could study *Moose, Bear, Beaver and Eagles in the Superior National Forest*. The Great Smoky Mountain Institute at Tremont, Tennessee, bridges the generation gap with the course, *Exploring the Smokies with your Grandchildren*. The University of South Florida offered *Wildlife Across Florida* while the University of Arizona at Tucson had three courses to acquaint you with animals of the desert: *Creatures of the Night, Desert Creepy Crawlies*, and *Mammals of the Southwest*.

You or a younger member of your family can take advantage of other wildlife education opportunities. City zoos and local nature centers, mentioned earlier, offer natural science outreach programs. The National Audubon Society presents environmental education programs for young people and families through the efforts of more than five hundred Audubon chapters nationwide as well as six regional centers.

The Girl Scouts of the United States of America and the Boy Scouts of America also offer wildlife education. Both include a wildlife badge in their accomplishment ladders as well as extensive training for their adult leaders.

A hands-on experience in the outdoors is guaranteed to a high school or college student who signs up with the Student Conservation Association for a summer. The high schoolers work to enhance animal habitats, improve trails, and clear brush at national and state parks, forests, and refuges. College students use their summer vacation to serve as resource assistants, performing such duties as cataloging museum specimens or collecting biological data for wildlife investigators in the field.

College credits can be earned by taking part in exciting animal field studies sponsored by Wildlands Research, an extended education unit of San Francisco State University. In one project the enrollees joined a trained wildlife biologist to monitor the movements of free-roaming red wolves at Alligator River National Wildlife Refuge in North Carolina. They learned how to identify wolf signs and how to locate the wolves in the forest through the use of radiotelemetry—all to help reestablish the red wolf in its former southern habitat.

CHAPTER 4

Cultivating the Art of Observing Wildlife

Dusk was darkening the forest when Marge and I hiked out to an oxbow in McDonald Creek in the southern part of Glacier National Park in Montana.

The ranger at the visitor center had told us this would be a good spot to use our wildlife observation skills. In addition, he said, beaver had been building a lodge on this quiet backwater of the creek.

We found a comfortable spot under a pine tree atop a bluff, overlooking the still waters of the oxbow and the flowing creek beyond. It was like a balcony seat at a live animal show. At one side of the oxbow a large heap of branches marked the beaver lodge. We sat quietly, keeping our movements to a minimum. As evening descended on the oxbow and the small overgrown island at its center, we watched, listened—and waited.

The first sound we heard was a rustle on the forest floor a few feet from us. A golden mantled ground squirrel with stripes down its back (but none on its face as a chipmunk would have had) scurried down a tree trunk, zigzagged across the duff six feet in front of us, and disappeared around the base of another tree. Its movements reminded me of the freeze frames of a televised football game: it ran a few feet, stopped, looked around, then ran some more, until it reached a protected spot.

Down below us the only movements were the V-shaped waves of several ducks paddling leisurely in the still water. Then we noticed motion in the tall grass on the island. Out stepped a doe mule deer with two fawns.

The graceful animals grazed for a time, moving ahead step by step as they munched the grass, staying close together. After a while the doe led the way across a shallow arm of the oxbow, daintily stepping across its rocky bottom and into the meadow beyond.

Now the stillness of the evening was broken by the sounds of young voices. Three people in a rubber raft swung into view on the creek. We guessed it was a father and two sons out for a nature-watching trip. The sound of the intruders alerted the animals. The deer edged into the brush, just far enough to be out of sight. The ducks paddled into the overhanging grass along the edge of the creek. By the time the raft passed the oxbow all wildlife had disappeared. The occupants of the raft would see none of these animals as they drifted by—a lesson to us that humans must intrude gently into the animal world.

Quiet returned. As we watched in the dimness a buck mule deer sporting a handsome set of antlers stepped out of the high grass along the far shore and onto the small island. After grazing for a while, it too waded across to the opposite side and bounded up the bank, following the same path used earlier by the doe and its fawns.

By now it was almost dark. Although we hadn't seen the beavers we had come to observe, we had a rewarding

A young visitor has moved dangerously close to a bull bison grazing at Badlands National Park. At the moment the animal's loosely hanging tail indicates it is not alarmed, but rangers advise staying at least one hundred yards away from these powerful and unpredictable animals. Use your binoculars to bring a big animal like this "up close."

glimpse into the animal world without interfering with its natural rhythm.

Observing animals in the wild is an art—and a challenge. Birds, who stay safe from harm high in a tree or in the air, can afford to advertise themselves by being visible and by wearing bright plumage. Not so the mammals. Animals that live on or under the ground make a career out of staying out of sight, disguising themselves, and blending into surroundings. Mammals that are easily seen don't survive long.

Fur, a feature that is unique to mammals, is usually brown or gray. The snowshoe hare's fur coats even change with the season—brown in the summer, white in the winter—to achieve a year-round camouflage.

Sometimes a pattern supplements the protective coloration. A deer fawn is born with splotches of white on its light brown coat. The pattern helps the young animal blend in with the high grass or brush until it gets old enough to forage for itself.

Some animals avoid the light of day entirely. Such nocturnal animals seek out food under cover of darkness, which protects them from potential predators. Foraging at night also allows them to avoid the heat of the day and work when it is cool. Mice, for example, scurry around at night, led by their keen sense of smell. Skunks patrol campgrounds looking for leftovers after the human campers have turned in. Owls, who possess 20/20 vision or better at night, swoop out of the darkness to snatch unwary prey.

Other animals have highly developed senses of sight, smell, taste, hearing, or touch. The pronghorn, the graceful speedster of the prairie, can see an approaching intruder a mile away. The black bear's acute sense of smell can locate any food stored at a campsite. A prairie dog senses the vibrations made by a person or animal walking atop its burrow.

The wildlife observer needs to develop techniques to outwit these animal defense mechanisms, to overcome the natural tendency of almost every mammal to stay out of sight to protect itself and its young.

As you drive park tour roads or hike refuge trails, learn to be an outdoor detective. Look for clues that improve your chances of observing wild animals. Discover some of the American Indian's tracking skills, which often determined whether or not he would eat dinner.

One of the first tricks to learn is the art of silence. Stillness comes hard to those of us accustomed to communicating freely, to talking out our actions, to having sounds all around us. Since wild animals are sensitive to unusual sounds, smells, or movements, you'll need to do everything you can to blend in with your surroundings—including becoming part of the silence of the outdoors.

Bill McRae, a noted wildlife photographer, emphasizes the importance of staying quiet and exercising patience. He describes how a stealthy approach to a group of deer enabled him to get the photographs his editor wanted.

"One morning, a half-hour before sunrise, I spotted five mule deer bucks in velvet high on a ridge," he wrote. "By approaching slowly at oblique angles, I was in position to start using my 400mm lens as the first golden rays of sunlight flooded the scene.

"Each time the deer seemed skittish I backed off for a while, and in a couple of hours I was accepted as one of the boys. When they retreated to a cool aspen grove to bed down about 9 A.M., I went too, and actually took a nap about fifteen feet from the largest buck, which intermittently slept and chewed its cud.

"When they got up at 5 P.M. and headed for a lake, I again tagged along and got excellent pictures of them drinking and wading. No doubt the deer would have run off had I rushed them, but by taking my time and by showing respect, I was able to photograph them doing what deer do naturally."

Just as a dog uses its superb sense of smell to follow a trail, you need to use your best tracking senses: eyesight, hearing, and intelligence. Train yourself to read the clues animals leave for you.

As you look for evidence of animal activity, you have one factor in your favor. Many animals are creatures of habit. Once familiar with a food or water source they tend to return to it again and again. Such repeat trips create visible trails.

You may spot the tunnel a vole has burrowed in the grass or a path through the brush where deer have matted down the vegetation on the way to a stream. You might notice broken branches in a berry patch where a bear has been feeding.

Watch for places where marsh and field meet woods or forest. Look into creek beds and river bottoms and up valleys. Less inhabited lakes and old logging roads, fire lanes, power company transmission lines, and backcountry trails—these make good wildlife habitats.

When you find a place that seems to have a good deal of wildlife activity, you might stake it out to see what comes by. Build a simple blind with branches and brush downwind from the trail or feeding area you've found so that animals do not pick up your scent. The blind will keep you out of sight and permit you to observe the animals without their sensing your presence. It will also protect you from sun, wind, or rain while you wait.

You will be less noticeable in clothes of muted colors—like the animals themselves. Avoid contrasting color shades and loose-fitting garments that could slap against a bush or a tree.

Be ready to freeze should you see something move. Many animals see only in black and white rather than color and detect potential enemies mainly by seeing their movement. If you freeze, you become part of their visual background and become difficult for them to see. Every wild animal has its "flight distance," the minimum distance it requires between itself and an intruder. If an observer moves within an animal's flight distance, it will ease away or flee.

Marge and I did some unplanned stalking one evening on a nature trail at Cades Cove in the Great Smokies. Walking carefully to avoid stepping on twigs or branches that could snap, and maintaining complete silence, we saw a blur of movement deep in the woods to our right. We froze and took a look in that direction.

Three mule deer browsed among the trees and shrubs. We were downwind from the animals so that at first they did not pick up our scent or catch our movements. We watched for several minutes as the deer made crackling sounds with their hooves while nibbling on the leaves. Then a deer looked up and spotted us. All three pricked up their ears but continued to graze: we were outside their flight distance. After some fifteen minutes we simply walked on up the trail, leaving the deer to continue feeding.

Animal Signs

You will often see hints of an animal before you see the animal itself. Two kinds of animal signs are common: those you see and those you hear. Let's take a look at some of the clues you will find, signs that mean that you're in the animal's neighborhood.

Food Gathering

One of the best ways to see wildlife is to know an animal's food-gathering habits.

A close relationship exists between animals and plants—for a good reason. Animals constantly search for food to eat—and the plant world provides most of it. The least popular items on the animal menu are algae, fungi, lichens, and mosses. Seed plants, grasses, shrubs, and berry bushes are high on the list, sustaining many an animal—from mice to moose. A few plants even take their name from the animal that relies on it, for example, buffalograss, rabbitbush, deervetch, and duckweed.

Plants can provide a substantial diet, as anyone who patronizes a health food store will recognize. Many seeds contain up to twenty-five percent protein compared to fourteen percent protein for chicken eggs and nineteen percent for sirloin of beef.

By watching for wildlife in areas where preferred foods are abundant you are more likely to find the hungry animal. In spring, animals look for buds, tree flowers, and fresh, tender vegetation. By summer, mature plants and trees bear succulent fruit for animal diets.

Fall is the season when plants go to seed. Nuts and

fruit are abundant. Many animals such as bears eat ravenously to store up the fat layer that will sustain them over the long winter. In winter, of course, food becomes scarce and animals depend on fat stored in their bodies or food tucked away in dens. They also eat the few shrubs and leaves that still remain above the snow line.

Learn how the seasons affect an animal's food-gathering habits. In the West, when snow covers the mountains, elk, mule deer, and mountain sheep move down into valleys where grass still grows. Meanwhile, rodents such as the marmot and pika are busy storing grass and forbs under rocks where they will be available for winter munching.

Squirrels, chipmunks, and kangaroo rats set aside nuts, dry fruit, and seeds. Beavers drag tree branches from the shore to their lodge where they store them underwater to provide a winter food source to feed on—even under the ice.

Plants that serve animals as sources of food often provide cover as well. Cover is the shelter an animal needs to stay alive. It protects an animal from rain, wind, summer heat, predators, and especially the combination of cold and wind.

Hedgerows and the edges between field and forest are promising places to look for wildlife because these habitats offer both food and cover to animals. Here grow tasty bushes like the wild rose, hazelnut, elderberry, and chokecherry; and plants like goldenrod, aster, poke-weed, milkweed, and broomsedge. Moreover, the place where a field and forest merge offers safety to an animal, such as a deer. If danger threatens, the deer can easily melt into the forest and escape.

Farmers' crops also attract wildlife. Some farmers admit that wildlife can help as well as hurt their crops. Studies have demonstrated that the damage from animals to farm crops is often less than that from frost, drought, erosion, insects, or plant diseases. What's more, animals often compensate for the loss of crops they eat by helping to control undesirable weeds and insects.

Tracks

Wildlife watchers, like good detectives, should take a good look around for footprints. In the animal world, they're called *tracks*.

The track of each animal species is unique. The paw print of a black bear is entirely different from the dispersed dots of a rabbit. A moose's track looks like a larger version of a white-tailed deer's, which makes sense because the moose and deer are members of the same family. A beaver track clearly reveals that the animal has webbed feet for swimming. A point to remember: the front track of an animal is often distinct in size and shape from its rear track.

Good places to look for tracks are along muddy

The track of a red fox shows clearly in a sand dune at Assateague National Seashore in Maryland. **Photo by Richard Frear, National Park Service.**

stream banks where animals come to drink, in patches of damp earth where footsteps leave an impression, in desert sand, or in snow. Tracks are often the only visible evidence of nocturnal creatures. A tiny print that looks like a human hand would tip you off that you had been visited during the night by a raccoon.

Naturalists divide mammals into three groups according to their tracks:

1. Animals that walk flat-footed.   These creatures press down firmly with all four feet. Flat-footed walkers have longer hindfoot tracks than forefoot tracks. Among them are the bear, skunk, beaver, porcupine, and raccoon.

2. Animals that walk on their toes.   Wolves, foxes, coyotes, mountain lions, and bobcats literally walk on their toes.

3. Animals that walk on their toenails.   As hoofed mammals evolved, they lost several toes and developed instead two large toenails or hooves. Deer, elk, moose, pronghorn, mountain sheep, and goats all have hooves for feet. The hereditary remains of two earlier toes protrude above the hoof on the rear of the animal's leg. These are called "dewclaws" and can become part of the deer's track when it walks in soft ground or snow. The dewclaw helps support the deer's weight, preventing it from sinking in soft ground, thus leaving an impression.

The more practiced you become at tracking, the more information you will be able to deduce about an animal's actions.

You might even be able to tell a white-tailed deer's track from that of a mule deer. The white-tailed deer is a "quiet walker" whose hind feet often step into the same track as the forefeet, producing two petal-shaped imprints. When the ground is soft, smaller circular marks are made behind the petal shapes by the dewclaws. The tip of a buck's track points slightly outward, while a doe's points straight ahead.

The hoof marks of a mule deer are firmer than those of a white-tailed deer because the mule deer places its foot more solidly on the ground when walking. The distinction becomes apparent when the muley bounds away from a threat. Then its tracks reflect a stiff-legged bounding action—as if the animal were bouncing on springs. The track shows all four feet close together with the hindfeet actually ahead of the forefeet—a distinctive sign to look for.

Black bears leave signs other than tracks. One day at Grand Teton National Park we spotted bear scratchings, deep claw marks eight to ten feet up the trunk of a tree, made by a bear to mark its territory.

The bear stands on its hind legs and gashes the tree bark with its teeth and claws. When another bear comes along, it sniffs the tree, looks at the marks, and tries to scratch higher up the trunk. If it cannot, it moves on to a territory where it can be the largest bear. On the other hand, if the first bear discovers that a larger bear has marked higher up the tree, it may move to another territory.

Male bears leave an additional calling card. They smear mud on a tree trunk with a paw, then scrape their backs against the muddy trunk so that some of their hair pulls out and adheres to the mud. Another male, reading this sign, may decide that one male in the territory is enough; he may move on to an unmarked area. Or a female who reads the sign may decide to stay in the area if breeding time is approaching.

To give you a head start in recognizing animal tracks and droppings, illustrations of each have been included with the animal descriptions in chapters 5 through 9. You will be a giant step ahead of other park and refuge visitors if you familiarize yourself with the animal tracks and signs you expect to find.

For additional details on tracks and droppings you might look for a widely recognized and comprehensive book on animal tracks, *A Field Guide to Animal Tracks*, written and illustrated by the late Olaus J. Murie. Murie lived in Grand Teton National Park for twenty-five years, and until his death in 1963 was one of America's leading mammologists and field biologists. In his book he describes and includes detailed drawings of the tracks and scat of most of North America's common mammals.

Droppings

Another sign you shouldn't overlook are droppings, or scat. Expert trackers often use a combination of scat and tracks to identify an animal.

Droppings, of course, vary with the size of the animal and with its diet. Bison scat—the familiar pie-shaped "buffalo chips" of the prairie—are about the size and shape of the popular frisbie. A black bear's scat consists of cylindrical pieces perhaps one and one-half inches in diameter.

Skunk droppings are about three inches long and a half inch in diameter. Droppings of hoofed mammals like deer, mountain sheep, and mountain goats all take the form of rounded pieces, or pellets. Droppings that are neatly covered over with dirt or leaves were probably left by a member of the cat family; cats are fastidious about hiding their excretions. A porcupine gnaws deep sections out of the trunk of its favorite tree, leaving mounds of droppings at the base of the tree or at the entrance to its den.

Owl pellets (food wastes the owl regurgitates) teach so many lessons that they make a favorite unit for nature study class projects. You will find the smooth-shaped pellets beneath a tree where an owl has roosted; come back quietly to the same tree after dark and you may be able to observe the owl at work. If you dissect an owl pellet you will most likely find within it tiny pieces of fur and bone, the undigested parts of the bird's last victim.

Home

Another important clue that will help you locate an animal in the wild is its home.

Animal homes come in all shapes and sizes depending on the size of the animal, the climate, available building materials, and the skill of the builder. Like our own abodes, animal homes provide protection from predators, shelter from harsh weather, storage space for food, and a place to raise young.

To determine what animal lives in a shelter you've discovered, look at the home's floor plan and neighborhood. Note its location, elevation, placement and sizes of entrances and exits, and paths or runways leading to it.

An oval hole in open grassland might be a badger's home. The busy badger is a prodigious digger, excavating underground burrows up to thirty feet long and five feet deep. Using its two-inch claws the badger can dig a tunnel rapidly, piling up dirt behind its body, then spreading debris in the shape of a fan in front of the entrance. Since this creature works and hunts at night and sleeps in the day, you probably won't see the badger itself—but you can easily recognize its place of residence.

A nest of leaves and twigs high in a tree is most likely a squirrel's summer nest. Well-fed squirrels may produce two litters a year, one in February or March, another in midsummer. The summer litter is raised in a treetop nest of leaves lined with soft, shredded bark, the winter litter in a leaf-filled cavity in the trunk of a tree. With careful observation, you may see a squirrel taking food to a nest to feed its babies.

A circular area of matted-down grass at the edge of a thicket may tip you off to a deer's home. Deer spend most of the daytime lying in a bed of grass, resting and chewing their cud, the undigested portion of food they ate hurriedly. The ideal location for a deer's bed is atop a slope with an unobstructed view of an intruder's approach.

The animal that is probably easiest to locate by its homesite is the beaver. A master workman, the beaver builds a dome-shaped lodge of sticks and logs plastered with mud. The beaver's dam, built nearby, backs up water around the lodge like a moat providing a water barrier for a medieval castle.

It's pretty obvious when a beaver is working nearby. While walking a trail along a creek in Rocky Mountain National Park, Marge and I came upon an entire clearing of aspen trees. Each tree, two to three inches in diameter, had been neatly chopped by the sharp-toothed beaver and dragged down an embankment, where it would be cut into sections to be added to a dam or lodge.

Sounds

As we gathered with other campers at dusk one day at the isolated Sage Creek campground in Badlands National Park, we heard a long howl that ended with a *yip-yip-yow-oo-oo*. The sound came from a nearby wooded area and carried clearly in the still evening air. We soon realized it was produced by that symbol of the West, the coyote.

The coyote's howl is more than a song at the end of the day. The howl and accompanying bark are part of its hunting strategy.

For example, two coyotes, a hunting pair, will approach a prairie dog town and stand perfectly still, out of sight of the rodents, for several minutes, watching. Then one of the coyotes walks through the colony yapping continuously. The frightened prairie dogs dive into their holes. After the prairie dogs have gone below ground, the second coyote moves quietly to a hole where one of the prairie dogs has disappeared. Meanwhile, the first coyote continues yapping as it passes through the town. As the noise fades away the prairie dogs reappear for a look around. When a rodent pops up at the hole where the second coyote waits, the coyote grabs its meal.

The prairie dog's fellow rodent, the marmot, signals danger with a shrill, piercing whistle. The marmot perches on a high rock in its mountain home to keep an eye out for intruders. When the danger signal sounds, all marmots in the colony run to their dens beneath the rocks, reappearing only when they hear the all-clear signal—a lower pitched whistle.

The beaver's warning signal is even more distinctive. This creature raises its flat tail up over its back, then brings it down with such force on the surface of the water that the resulting *thwack* can be heard for half a mile on a quiet night. The sound causes all beavers in the area to race for water and dive to safety.

An elk's bugle is another sound you may hear in elk country during the fall rut. It is the male elk that does the bugling, warning other males away from his hard-earned harem of females, and perhaps trying to impress the females as well.

At Wind Cave National Park we went on a nocturnal walk to learn more about animal sounds. Ranger Margaret Marshall, a summer seasonal employee who makes her home in Westchester County, New York, carried a flashlight, its lens covered with red plastic. The red light, she explained, is invisible to most animals; a standard flashlight beam would have alerted them to a person's presence.

Our group of ten wildlife enthusiasts climbed a path from a parking area to a broad meadow. Margaret found a comfortable spot along a trail and suggested we sit down in the gathering darkness and keep our voices low.

She talked quietly about animals we might hear around us that were hidden in the darkness. Since many rodents come out of their holes after nightfall, she said, coyotes often prowl the meadow in hopes of finding a mouse or a vole. Owls, with their acute night vision, hunt their prey in the dark.

As a bonus on this clear, cool August night Margaret also called our attention to the night sky, a sparkling canopy of stars. Together we picked out our favorite constellations and galaxies, such as the Milky Way, and watched as several meteor showers cut bright paths across the sky.

By now it was so black you could not see the person beside you. Margaret pulled a cassette tape recorder from her trailpack. A coyote's howl blasted out as she turned the recorder to full volume. She played the howl several times; it reverberated from the nearby woods. Then we listened.

No response. She played it again and we listened. Still nothing.

"Sometimes we're successful and sometimes we're not," she admitted. "A number of times we have gotten a coyote to answer. But who knows, there may not be a coyote around tonight."

Then she played the *who-o-o-o, who-o-o-o* of the great horned owl several times but again was unable to get a response from the big birds.

Although Margaret was unsuccessful at getting any feedback, our group agreed that simply hearing the calls played in the wild would help us to identify a coyote or an owl if we heard one.

"Knowing some animal sounds would definitely have helped a lady we had here recently," Margaret concluded with a smile. She told us about the woman who asked her one morning if there were any big lions in the park. She had heard deep growls during the night that scared her half to death and she was unable to sleep. Margaret assured her that there were no lions in the vicinity but that a bison herd was grazing a mile or so away. Undoubtedly, she told the frightened visitor, what she had heard was a bull bison bellowing to tell other males to stay out of its territory.

We had another experience in animal communication at Roberts Prairie Dog Town in Badlands National Park. There, a stretch of flat greenish prairie is pockmarked by what looks like miniature bunkers: prairie dog burrows.

Walk out among the burrows and you soon become aware of a series of high-pitched chirps, first from one direction, then from another.

The chirps are evidence of a highly developed alarm system (which can occasionally be circumvented by the wily coyote). Any of the rodents sitting atop a burrow entrance can act as a sentry, watching for signs of danger.

As soon as a sentry spotted us, it began a steady *chirp-chirp-chirp* as we moved closer, then dived down its hole. As we continued through the burrows we heard another chirp twenty or thirty feet farther into the colony; another prairie dog had passed along the warning. Whatever approach we chose, the chirping extended ahead of us as various prairie dogs warned their neighbors. We continued to hear the warning chirps but only rarely could get close enough to even see the elusive rodents with our binoculars: the warning system was working!

We later learned that by staying in our motor home and using it as a blind, we could have watched the prairie dogs close at hand. The sounds of our conversation and the vibrations from our footsteps were thwarting our efforts to see these clever rodents.

Other Signs

As you become a more practiced tracker you will notice other clues to the animals in the neighborhood.

Broken branches on berry bushes indicate that bears have been feeding. The browse line at a forest's edge will tip you off to hungry deer in the area.

In bison country you may see trees or even telephone poles where bison have rubbed their horns and flanks. Some trees even bear a "rub line," a worn spot where an animal has scratched itself numerous times. You might even find some kinky black bison hairs caught in the tree bark. Look for bison wallows—open areas of exposed earth where the big animals have rolled to get a dirt bath.

Finally, an obvious but unpleasant indication of the presence of animals is a road kill. Many animals are killed by vehicles as they cross roadways and railways. Nocturnal animals are particularly vulnerable because they are active at night when motorists may not see them. On one ten-mile stretch of highway through open prairie west of Hot Springs, South Dakota, we noted the remains of a porcupine, a snake, and two bobcats.

Weather and Wildlife Watching

Like people, most animals are not anxious to forage in nasty weather. Rainy or snowy days are not particularly good for wildlife watching—either for you or for the animals.

It is helpful to cultivate a woodsman's sense of the weather before you begin a day's wildlife venture. Some basic meteorology may prevent you from heading out on a day when creatures are scarce.

Weather forecasters will tell you that generally no major change occurs in weather without a change in wind direction. Typically, winds that blow from the southwest, northwest, or north tend to bring fair weather; winds from the south, east, or northeast tend to bring rain, snow, or sleet.

Storms often accompany low pressure systems (areas where barometer readings are low) and generally move across the United States from west to east. In a low pressure system, winds circulate counterclockwise. You can determine from the direction the wind is blowing whether a storm is moving past you. Wind from the south usually indicates you are in the storm's southeast quadrant, or leading edge. As the storm moves through an area, the wind shifts to the west, then to the northwest, and finally to the north as the weather clears.

Clouds, too, give important clues to upcoming weather. Cumulus, the white, fluffy clouds that are usually high in the sky at four thousand to five thousand feet, are fair-weather clouds. They usually mean a sunny day—unless they bunch up and enlarge vertically to form a towering formation with a darkening base. This vertical accumulation often occurs in late afternoon on a hot day and probably precedes rain, possibly a thunderstorm.

If you're caught on the trail with a thunderstorm threatening, you can determine whether the storm is approaching or moving away. Count the seconds between a flash of lightning and its accompanying clap of thunder. Each five seconds represents one mile between you and the storm. Note several such time intervals and you will know whether the storm is moving toward you or away from you.

If you want to learn more about different cloud formations or safety precautions in storms, the U.S. Weather Service has published two inexpensive booklets you can order from the Superintendent of Documents, U.S. Government Printing Office, Washington, DC 20402. They are: *Clouds* (003-014-00016-9) and *Watch Out, Storms Ahead! Owlie Skywarn's Weather Book* (003-017-00513-50).

Then, too, you may sense a change in weather from the actions of the animals you're observing. Elk and deer descend from mountains at the approach of a storm, especially if snow is likely. If deer and moose, who normally graze in the early morning or late afternoon, are feeding avidly at midday, you can anticipate bad weather. If you hear a coyote howl in midmorning, you can bet a storm is coming.

Equipment and Clothing

First of all, rangers emphasize, every wildlife observer should take along two intangibles: curiosity and patience. Curiosity will motivate you. It will help you appreciate the natural world around you. Patience will give you the staying power to stake out and stalk the animals you hope to see. These traits should go along on any wildlife adventure. Fortunately they do not take up any space. As for other equipment, only a few things are essential.

Binoculars.   You'll need a good pair of binoculars to get a close-up view of the animals you locate. Rangers recommend 7 X 35, 7 X 50, or 8 X 40 binoculars. The first number is the magnification power of the lens; the second number is the lens diameter (the larger the lens diameter, the more light enters, giving you a better view of the subject in dim light). A good rule of thumb is to buy binoculars whose lens diameter is about five times its magnification power. Consider getting lenses that are color-coated, which reduces glare. Consider also the weight: the lighter, the better, because you will have them around your neck all day.

Field guide.   Another worthwhile item to carry is a good field guide for identifying animals. Two that we like are: *Mammals* from the Roger Tory Peterson Field Guide Series, by William H. Burt, with illustrations by the late Richard P. Grossenheider; and the *Complete Field Guide to North American Wildlife*, assembled by Jay Ellis Ransom. The Burt guide's advantage is that it fits into a trouser pocket or trail pack. It includes mammals only, although other Peterson guides cover reptiles and amphibians and, of course, birds. The Ransom guide is broader in scope, cataloging not only mammals but birds, reptiles, amphibians, fish, and mollusks. It comes in two volumes, for eastern or western North America.

Footgear. The next item to consider is what to wear on your feet. You'll need a good pair of hiking shoes that you can wear all day, shoes that keep your feet comfortable, warm, and dry.

For a day hike in good weather on one of the improved hiking trails in a national park, national forest, or wildlife refuge, a low athletic shoe with a good arch support is fine. These shoes are popular, readily available, lightweight, and have a good gripping tread for climbing over rocks. They normally have sides of canvas or leather that allow your feet to breathe so that they don't become overheated.

For a longer hike or for traversing rough terrain, rangers recommend a true hiking boot. Manufacturers are now selling a hiking boot that weighs less than the traditional cowhide hiking boot with the lug sole often referred to as the "waffle stomper." The newer boot sandwiches a microporous film between its inner and outer layers of leather and fabric to produce a boot that is waterproof yet allows your foot to breathe. A high-top boot of this type provides good ankle support and keeps feet dry in wet terrain or on rainy days. Its sole is also easier on the trail—a concern for rangers who find that the lug-soled boots wear deep ruts in park trails.

Another trail shoe particularly good for hikes in wet weather is the waterproof gum shoe, popularly called a "duck." This shoe can be a low, high-top, or knee-high boot. It has a leather upper and a heavy rubber wraparound sole with a textured tread. The boot is warm and comfortable for hiking but doesn't breathe; feet may become hot after hiking a while. But the offsetting benefit is that "ducks" keep your feet completely dry even after a day of hiking in wet terrain.

Clothing. What you wear for a day of wildlife watching essentially depends on common sense, the environment, and the season. But a few guidelines passed along by rangers who have spent many hours in the field might prove helpful.

In general, the best insulation for clothing is provided by natural fibers. Cotton is the top choice for hot weather because it gives protection from the sun while allowing air to flow through the fabric to your skin. Wool shirts and pants are most effective at providing warmth in cold weather and protection from rain or snow. Wool absorbs more moisture than any other fabric yet still retains its warmth. Goose down offers the warmest insulation for jackets. Cotton and wool materials are also quieter in the woods than synthetic materials.

Synthetic fabrics, however, have values and uses that make them indispensable for certain outdoor clothing. Raingear made with the same microporous film layer as that used in the lightweight boot is becoming popular. Known in the trade as PTFE and sold under trade names such as Goretex or Klimate, this breakthrough fabric has ushered in a new generation of outdoor clothing. Although it is porous and permits perspiration vapor to flow through it, rain does not penetrate it. The microporous layer is sandwiched between outer and inner layers such as cotton or nylon. Rainpants and ponchos of this material are lightweight and fold easily into small packages when you're not wearing them.

Since the weather is often cool in the morning and warmer at midday, rangers recommend that you dress in layers. Start with wool or wool-blend socks and warm underwear. Add a pullover sweater over a long-sleeved shirt, then a parka and a hat, or a poncho or rainsuit if rainy weather is likely. Take along gloves even in summer in case it turns cold in the evening. A hat is recommended—it will shed rain, keep your hair from blowing, and help keep insects away.

If in doubt, dress too warmly. You can always remove layers and carry them in your trail pack. We proved the value of this advice one day watching the annual migration of raptors at Hawk Mountain near Reading, Pennsylvania. Marge and I were warm as we walked the trail to the overlook, but needed to add wool hat and gloves when we were exposed to the wind at the bird watching spot.

Here are a few other items you may want to tuck in your trail pack along with your lunch:

Camera.   Whether and when to put aside wildlife watching in favor of wildlife photography requires some careful consideration. Photographing wild animals is an art unto itself, demanding great patience, photographic expertise, and bulky telephoto lenses. But you can easily bring along a well-equipped compact camera and record some of your memorable experiences without disturbing the animals you're watching or adding much weight to your pack.

Tape recorder.   If you want to try to duplicate the wildlife listening experiences of the rangers, bring your own tape recorder and try it. You can purchase cassettes of owl, coyote, moose, or elk sounds, among others, or you can tape animal sounds right in the field.

Spotting scope.   Short telescopes called spotting scopes are available at sporting goods or camera stores. Unlike binoculars, which are easy to hold and focus, spotting scopes need to be supported to be steady enough to look through. The scope's advantage is its greater magnification, which gives you a closer view of the animal. At the same time, your field of view is smaller, which often makes it harder to bring the animal into your sight. A scope works well for wildlife viewing from a car or recreational vehicle or mounted on a tripod at a blind.

Insect repellant.   Biting insects thrive in many parts of the country. Your first line of defense is your long-sleeved shirt and a hat. Add a headnet if you need to. Bring along a repellant to ward off mosquitos, black flies, and deer flies. When you are bitten, apply ammonia or damp baking soda to relieve the itching.

Canteen. When hiking on hot days, in the desert, or at high altitudes, it is important to replenish the fluid you perspire from your body. Rangers advise day hikers to carry a canteen of water with them on any walk longer than two hours. They also warn against drinking from any stream; even when the water is crystal clear, there's no guarantee it contains no contaminants.

Other items you should tuck into your trail pack include a pocket knife, compass, and map of the area, as well as a first aid and snake bite kit.

Into the Field

We got a chance to try our animal stalking techniques one day at Wind Cave National Park. Rich Klukas, the staff research biologist, had told us of recent mule deer sightings in a certain draw, or low valley. He emphasized that the mule deer has a keen sense of hearing and that an observer needs to approach silently.

It was noon on a warm, sunny day. We walked through knee-high grass on one slope of the draw. Realizing that a deer would most likely be resting and chewing its cud at this hour of the day, we peered carefully beneath the numerous thickets of chokecherry.

Then we saw it—a splotch of tan under a bush—and signaled each other to stay quiet. Looking through our binoculars, we could see a doe mule deer lying at the front edge of a large thicket. The deer had already spotted us—both ears stood straight up on its head, which was turned in our direction. A mule deer's ears can follow a sound such as our footsteps like radar antennas. The two ears can even swivel in opposite directions to pick up sounds coming from different angles.

We took a few steps, trying to edge a little closer. Suddenly, out of the thicket leaped a fawn, playfully bounding away up the slope, disappearing into a more distant clump of bushes. The doe quickly rose to its feet and made its way to the second thicket where its fawn waited.

We moved no farther, but sat down under a pine tree to observe. Soon the fawn appeared beside the doe and its mother nuzzled it protectively. The doe lay down once more, at the leading edge of the new thicket where it could keep an eye on us. The mule deer's distant vision is mediocre but it can detect motion instantly.

The fawn occasionally stepped out of the bushes to graze, then bounded back under cover again. The doe maintained its sentry position, its head turned directly toward us. There it remained, vigilant and alert, until we retreated from our observation point a half-hour later, pleased with ourselves for having followed the clues of habitat to a mule deer's lair.

CHAPTER
5

Wildlife of
the Appalachians and
Eastern Woodlands

An excellent place to observe the diversity of animals living in the Eastern woodlands is along Skyline Drive, which twists along a ridge through Shenandoah National Park in Virginia.

As we drove this route slowly one evening we observed roadside visitors: a chipmunk that disappeared into a stone wall, a gray squirrel that scurried up a tree.

Farther up the road, cars were pulled over to the shoulder. We knew what that meant—a deer jam. Sure enough, a doe and her fawn grazed along the forest edge near the road, keeping a wary eye on those who tried to come too close. As we watched, a woman excitedly described a black bear crossing the drive a few miles back, a spot we had just passed without seeing a thing.

Such an everyday experience in Virginia is one small indication of the variety of animals that awaits you in this region of the country. Here the Appalachian Mountains stretch from Maine to Georgia, holding fertile valleys between their roughened peaks. Rivers cut through gaps in the mountains, flowing across the wide coastal plain to the Atlantic Ocean.

Woodlands cover much of the region, except where men have developed industries, built cities, and cleared trees to sow crops. Basswood, beech, buckeye, hickory, magnolia, maple, oak, and tulip poplar are the most abundant of 130 species of trees that grow in these deciduous forests (forests whose trees lose their leaves in autumn and grow them again in spring).

As the Eastern forest moves through its yearly cycle of change and growth, from the first leaves of spring to the blazing colors of autumn, the animals make good use of the abundant cover and their own protective coloration to stay out of sight.

Each animal has its own special place in the organization of forest life. Leaf-eating insects, insect-eating birds, and squirrels make their homes in the *canopy*, the uppermost layer of this temperate-zone forest. The green leaves of the canopy grow thick and lush in the intense sunlight to which they are exposed.

Squirrels, bobcats, bears, and others range through the next layer, the *understory*. Smaller trees—either shorter trees of the same canopy species or other varieties—make up this level.

Below the understory lies the *shrub* layer of forest growth, consisting of woody plants such as rhododendron and viburnum. Small animals—chipmunks, mice, and birds—find shelter and food among the branches of the forest shrubs.

Many other small creatures, as well as animals such as foxes and deer, thrive in the lowest level of forest vegetation, the *herb* layer. Grasses, wild flowers, ferns, and mosses, all considered herbs in scientific terms, create this layer.

Finally, the *forest floor*, littered with the dead leaves of autumn, provides the habitat for microscopic organisms and a multitude of other creatures, including the woodchuck and other burrowing animals.

Let's look through the eyes of rangers at some of the wild animals living in these habitats of the Appalachians and Eastern woodlands.

Black Bear

The black bear, one of the most powerful animals of this region, is also one of the most shy. You will undoubtedly be more interested in observing it than it will be in seeing you.

Ranger Amy Stodola at Shenandoah remembers one of the few times she has seen a black bear in an area of the park that wasn't wilderness.

"I was walking through a wooded area on an October day on my way to my residence when I spotted a bear braced in an apple tree, stuffing itself with ripe apples," she recalls. "Probably a female, I figured, since the heavier males don't usually climb trees but forage at ground level.

"As I watched, it stopped for a moment, then went after the remaining apples. I'm sure its hunger overcame its uneasiness at having a human being standing so close."

According to Park Superintendent Bill Wade, black bears had almost disappeared from the park when it was established fifty years ago. Settlers had cut much of the timber in the Blue Ridge Mountains prior to the establishment of the park, he explained. But, he noted, "the regrowth of the forest here has brought back hard mast (acorns and nuts), and berry bushes fill the meadows so that the bears now have a good food supply. A comprehensive bear study we recently completed estimates that

black bear

we now have five hundred to six hundred bears in the park."

To insure that the bears retain wild characteristics, the park managers discourage the animals from foraging for people's food in campgrounds. Bearproof trash cans prevent bears from raiding camper garbage or picnic areas. As a result, most black bears stay in the backcountry. Said Bill Wade, "Your best chance to see them is to get out on the trails that lead through good bear habitat."

Black bears are found in wooded mountain areas of the eastern, northcentral, and western United States. The black bear has a bulky body and stands on short, sturdy legs. A thick layer of fat under the skin and dense, coarse hair give it a round shape—and also make it possible for the bear to survive even the harshest winter weather.

It has rounded ears, small eyes, and a short tail. Most Eastern bears have a glossy black coat with a tan muzzle. In the West, black bears are sometimes cinnamon or bluish gray. We saw a bluish gray sow bear and her cub crossing a road at Glacier National Park, well away from its populated areas.

A bear walks on the soles of its feet, as do humans, and consequently its five-toed tracks resemble human footprints. It sniffs the air often as it wanders through forest and clearing. Any camper who has lost food not stored well out of a bear's reach can attest to its excellent sense of smell and good tree-climbing ability. Its hearing is moderately good but its eyesight is relatively poor. Despite its chunky appearance, a black bear can run as fast as a horse for a short distance.

Look for bears in forests of mixed hardwood and softwood trees where swamps, rivers, streams, or lakes lie nearby. Bears are opportunistic feeders, finding food mainly by scent. They keep to a largely vegetarian diet of berries, mast, roots, grasses, and the succulent leaves of hardwoods, although they will eat meat if they come upon it: amphibians, reptiles, small mammals, fish, dead animals, and human garbage. Keep an eye out for a log a bear has ripped open in search of insects and larvae.

Ranger/Naturalist Pat Jamieson at Grand Teton National Park told us about a bear looking for a cache of pine nuts carefully set aside for the winter by a squirrel. The bear gulped down the squirrel's winter stash in one big slurp.

Bears wander a wide area in their endless search for food. Biologists estimate that home ranges are about twenty-seven square miles for males but only about five square miles for females. One male tagged and recaptured during the Shenandoah bear study was eventually found near Baltimore, Maryland, ninety-four miles away. Since bears are on the move primarily at night, a good time to look for them is at dusk. Except for sows, which forage with their cubs, bears usually forage alone.

Signs to look for are claw scratches on a tree trunk—bears mark trees along certain trails. A "bear tree" may be repeatedly clawed, bitten, and rubbed by several bears to notify others of their presence. Look also for rocks that have been turned over by a bear searching for grubs. Bear tracks and bear droppings, of course, are other signs.

Claw marks also may indicate that a bear has climbed a tree. Climbing a tree is a bear's primary means of defense and escape. It digs the claws of its hindfeet into the tree trunk, holding itself close to the tree with its front claws, then brings its hind legs up to dig in for a new grip, thrusting its front legs upward to pull itself farther up the trunk. Coming down, it claws at the bark as it slides down, leaving the long gashes that are telltale bear signs.

In winter, a black bear heads for a den site for a long winter's sleep. Look for likely den sites beneath a fallen tree, in a rock cave, in a hollow tree or stump, or in a dense thicket or grove of evergreens. A bear can wedge itself into a surprisingly small space—the average den size is 5½ feet long and 2 feet high. Sometimes the animal doesn't quite fit; a ranger at Rocky Mountain National Park reported seeing a black bear sleeping soundly, its head and front half squeezed under a rock overhang while its rump remained exposed to the elements.

The black bear, a semihibernator, is a sound winter sleeper, although it can be roused. True hibernators such as woodchucks and bats do not wake up until spring even if disturbed. A bear's heartrate slows by fifty to sixty percent, its body temperature drops, and it does not urinate or defecate during slumber. A pregnant female gives birth to two or three cubs in January or February while still in her den and not fully awake. She nurses and grooms her cubs while still in a semiconscious state. After the cubs have been weaned in August, they stay with their mother for a full year while she teaches them the ways of the wild.

White-tailed Deer

On another day at Shenandoah, we watched as a white-tailed fawn approached a doe grazing on a grassy hillside. When the fawn ducked its head beneath its mother's flank in an attempt to nurse, the doe raised one leg and gently kicked the fawn away, much to the amusement of our group of observers.

"That fawn is about six months old," said Sarah Webb, our ranger guide. "The doe is telling it to stop relying on mother's milk and get out and forage for itself."

Sarah went on to point out other behavior patterns

white-tailed deer

during an hour's twilight walk: how deer lick each other as a sign of affection, how a deer can leave its scent on a trail by rubbing the scent glands on its hind legs against a shrub or tree, how a deer pauses every so often as it grazes to raise its head and listen for sounds. "It can't hear very well while it's chewing," Sarah explained.

White-tailed deer are numerous today and are found throughout the East and Midwest as well as most of the West—although in the West its cousin the mule deer is predominant. By 1900 the large population of deer known to the first settlers had dwindled to some three to five hundred thousand. But opening up forest clearings that provide vegetation deer can eat, exterminating predators such as the mountain lion and wolf, and enforcing limits on hunting have restored the deer population to about fourteen million. The white-tailed deer remains the number one game species for hunters, whose bows and arrows and firearms kill some two million each year.

When visiting a park or refuge, ask the rangers where you are most likely to see deer. At Shenandoah, as noted, you will often observe some of the park's estimated six thousand white-tailed deer grazing along the grassy edge of Skyline Drive. At Great Smokies one of their favorite locations is the forest edge and meadows of the verdant Cades Cove area.

Each animal, like this white-tailed deer along the Skyline Drive in Shenandoah National Park, has its characteristic "flight distance." Should this mother and daughter move any closer, the doe would undoubtedly flee.

The white-tailed deer is herbivorous and finds a wide variety of things to eat, from mushrooms and lichens to fruits, nuts, and even fish and insects. A deer has the ability to select the choicest leaves on a plant and to bite them off at their most nutritious stage. Its keen sense of smell can locate mushrooms and acorns under leafy coverings.

In winter it eats acorns, grass, and twigs, but these are less nutritious than its summer diet; as a result a deer often loses considerable weight by spring. Be alert to notice nipped-off branches, as well as trees whose bark has been stripped away by a deer's sharp teeth.

A white-tailed deer's coat is reddish brown in summer. By winter it turns grayish brown and grows heavier. Tubular hairs provide good insulation; snow that falls on a deer's coat does not melt, proving how well its coat holds body heat.

The buck grows its trademark—a new set of antlers—each spring. Its antlers grow from the top of its head, fed by the "velvet," a skin containing tiny blood vessels that covers the growing antlers.

By early fall the antlers have attained their full growth. The supply of blood to the velvet ceases and the antlers harden into bone. The buck rubs the dried velvet off against trees and rocks, then polishes its weapons for potential use against rivals. You may come across shreds of velvet hanging from tree branches. After the fall rut, or mating season, the buck's antlers fall off, completing this remarkable yearly growth cycle.

A buck grows its first set of antlers when it is a yearling. These are straight "spikes," or single-forked antlers. With each succeeding year, the antlers of a healthy deer become larger and heavier with the addition of branches (or tines), until the animal reaches its prime. In old age, the antlers become smaller and are often malformed.

Bucks live apart from does except during mating season. In summer you will probably see doe-fawn groups and groups of older or younger bucks. When bucks get together, they become more aggressive, sparring with each other to practice for the rutting season.

White-tailed does usually have one or two fawns in the late spring. They nurse and wean their youngsters during the summer. Yearling males leave mothers after one year to forage on their own. Young does remain with mothers for another year before dispersing.

Red and Gray Foxes

When we visited the headquarters of the Chincoteague National Wildlife Refuge in coastal Virginia, Outdoor Recreation Planner Jim Kenyon listed red fox among the animals protected within the refuge. But on this late afternoon when we walked the circular tour road wind-

red fox

grey fox

ing through a fragrant pine forest, we were more intent on seeing rarer animals—the endangered Delmarva Peninsula fox squirrel and the tiny sika deer.

All at once a blur of movement far up the road caused Marge and me to stop and remain motionless. A red fox approached, trotting along the road's edge, nose close to the ground, sniffing, heading toward us. Fifty feet away, it caught sight of us intruders and skidded to an abrupt stop. One appraising look and it turned into the woods, still sniffing but now and then throwing a piercing glance in our direction. Sensing no threat because we did not move, the fox simply circled around us at a safe distance, trotted back to the road, and continued its stalking.

Unlike many wild animals, the red fox actually appears to have increased in numbers in the United States since the first European settlers arrived. It is now the most abundant and widespread fox in North America. Before colonial times, only gray foxes were common in dense Eastern forests. But when farmers cleared land, they provided the open fields and wood edges the red fox likes. Cultivation of the land also encouraged the spread of voles, mice, and rabbits, the red fox's favorite prey. Meanwhile, the gray fox retreated to forested regions.

When threatened, the red fox runs for its life (which is why it has become the gentleman fox hunter's favorite quarry). A gray fox will climb a tree, and it is the only fox capable of doing so.

The red fox has lustrous reddish orange fur and a long, bushy white-tipped tail. The gray fox has a grizzled black and gray coat that is somewhat coarser than the red's. It has a long, bushy tail with a black streak running its length and a black tip.

Neither fox is a picky eater. A fox hunts under cover of darkness. In addition to the rodents it prefers, a fox will kill and eat almost anything the size of a rabbit or smaller: rats, birds, lizards, frogs, or an occasional farmer's chicken. In summer it also seeks out corn, nuts, berries, and, for dessert, a grasshopper. So acute is a fox's hearing that it can hear a mouse squeak from a distance of 150 feet. It is also a scavenger that will clean up a road kill. Sometimes a fox buries its kill, then comes back and eats it later.

Red foxes normally mate for life, while the gray fox only mates for one season. If you hear a fox bark in winter it may be the dog fox (a male red or gray fox) barking to locate a vixen (the female). When they find each other, the pair digs a new den or finds a suitable hollow log, rock crevice, or unused woodchuck burrow. The vixen readies the den while the dog fox continues to prowl its territory, seeking food and sleeping in the open, protected only by its bushy tail for a blanket. A good provider, it brings food back to the den for the vixen and pups.

Fox pups are born in early spring weighing about eight ounces. Their eyes remain closed after birth for eight to ten days. After nursing from their mother for four weeks, the pups emerge from the den. Both mother and father hunt to supply them with solid food until they are completely weaned in two or three months. The young ones leave the den area in mid-July or August but may forage with their parents for another month until the family disbands and the young foxes strike out on their own to claim a new territory.

Bobcat

Marge was the first to see the tawny feline. My eyes were glued to the winding mountain road as I maneuvered our motor home out of the isolated Cataloochee Cove in Great Smoky Mountains National Park.

"It's a bobcat—look!" she exclaimed. Ahead of us on the unpaved back road trotted the bobcat, its long back legs and shorter front ones giving it a bobbing gait. Stopping momentarily, it looked back over its shoulder, then veered over the steep road edge, disappearing into the mountainside brush. We were thrilled to catch a long-sought glimpse of this enterprising, nocturnal hunter.

Norm Whiddon, our campground host at Cataloochee, also had seen a bobcat recently. He had picked it up in the beam of his headlights in the predawn darkness as it sat on a fence along a park road.

Such sightings of the elusive bobcat are rare. This solitary hunter does most of its stalking either at night, early in the morning, or late in the evening. Barely twice the size of a house cat, the average bobcat weighs about twenty pounds and stands perhaps twenty-two inches high at the shoulder.

Its reddish brown fur is streaked and spotted with black; a ruff of fur surrounds its face. Pointed tufts of hair, which may serve as sound-amplifying antenna, bring its ears to a point. Its stubby six-inch tail is a distinctive feature—biologists say the female uses its tail in the same way a pronghorn does, lifting it to reveal the white fur beneath as a signal for her cubs to follow.

An efficient, wary predator, the bobcat is equipped with sharp senses of sight, smell, and especially hearing. It has large eyes that are well adapted to seeing in the dark. A bobcat's pupils are slit-shaped rather than round; they open wide to admit dim light.

Like most cats, the bobcat is a highly adaptive eater, taking maximum advantage of whatever prey is available. Favorite food items are rodents, mice, and squirrels but fish, lizards, and insects are also on the menu. Even remains of porcupines, mink, muskrat, skunk, frog, and fox have been found in their stomachs. While a bobcat is capable of taking down a sick or injured deer, it more often simply feeds on a deer that has already died or been killed.

bobcat

If you were to follow a bobcat's food-gathering tracks on a snowy day they might lead you up and down a mountainside, stopping at vantage points such as rock formations or low-leaning trees where the cat surveys its territory for prey. The trail might then lead across a stream on a log (although the bobcat is a good swimmer the log makes the crossing easy), and on to rock crevices, brushpiles, and thickets, each of which the bobcat checks out in search of a meal. Finally, the tracks might take you across a clear-cut area in the forest, an opening that attracts rats, mice, and other rodents and provides the bobcat good hunting.

Relying on its keen vision and hearing, the cat usually stalks to within a few feet of a prospective victim, then attacks with a rush. Like most felines, it lacks endurance and must catch its prey within a few strides or lose it. Sometimes the wily cat will lie in ambush along a game trail where it can nail dinner with a single pounce.

The tawny cat marks off a territory of several square miles or more depending on the existing food supply. A bobcat on a hunt will cover from three to seven miles in a twelve-hour period. Its trail is marked with urine and its scent about once every half mile.

The bobcat is a fierce fighter. If cornered, it hisses, spits, and snarls—and stands its ground against dogs or other antagonists many times its weight. To many it must seem larger than life. Rangers at Shenandoah report that a number of visitors each year mistakenly report seeing "mountain lions," sightings the rangers are convinced are actually bobcats.

Skunk

Seasonal Ranger Bill Fuchs had told us we could expect to find a skunk after dark in almost any campground or picnic area in Great Smoky Mountains National Park. We helped prove his point one night when we cooked dinner at the Chimneys picnic area deep in the park.

After dinner I stepped from the motor home in the darkness to dispose of our mealtime trash. Without those telltale white stripes down its back it might have escaped my notice as it nosed around the trash can. I stopped, softly called Marge, and together we watched the skunk waddle through our picnic area, once almost stepping on Marge's feet. Even the light from my flashlight didn't deter its single-minded search for food. It zigzagged around the area, nose to the ground, finally wandering away into the night.

Skunks adapt to many environments and are undiscriminating in their eating habits. They are found in all forty-eight of the contiguous United States. Look for them along edges between forests and fields rather than deep in the woods. Cornfields, too, attract skunks look-

skunk

ing for grasshoppers, grubs, and beetles; the cornstalks hide them from potential predators as they forage. The skunk's preference for campgrounds and picnic areas is proof that it has adapted to living around humans.

Although a member of the mink and weasel family, the skunk is not nearly as sleek and agile. In fact, its tiny head and arched body perched on stubby legs give it an ungainly appearance when walking. An adult skunk weighs between four and six pounds. Its fur is glistening black with a white band across the forehead that forks into two white stripes running down its back. A layer of soft underfur keeps the animal warm while the outer hairs shed rain. It walks flat on its feet and leaves a track that may remind you of a miniature bear track. Its senses of sight, smell, and hearing are fair to poor, but its sense of touch is acute.

A nocturnal prowler, the skunk may meander a quarter mile each night, eating insects, grubs, mice, shrews, grasses, leaves, buds, fruits, and, of course, the leftovers of humans.

The skunk has few predators—for the obvious reason. If threatened it disarms its enemy with an oily, foul-smelling liquid that it can spray up to fifteen feet. But it uses this ultimate weapon only as a last resort. First it drums its forefeet on the ground, snarls, arches its back, and raises its tail to bluff an antagonist. Only if the attacker persists does the skunk eject its scent through two nozzlelike ducts near its anus.

Skunks den in ground burrows, beneath buildings, in stumps, or in piles of wood or rocks. Often a skunk uses an abandoned woodchuck burrow. If no other site is available it digs its own burrow about three feet underground, which it connects to the surface with one or more tunnels. In this central chamber furnished with dry grass and leaves, it remains dormant all winter. A skunk may lose up to a third of its body weight before it ventures forth again in the spring.

Wild Turkey

If you're hiking through a mature forest interspersed with grassy clearings and you suddenly hear a *flop-flop-flop* of flapping wings, you have probably disturbed a flock of wild turkeys. One turkey probably sounded the alarm, which sounds like *putt*, signaling all birds to hide in the underbrush and remain motionless until the intruder disappeared.

The wild turkey is found today in woodlands throughout the United States, having recovered from the drastic reduction of its population by the ax, the plow, and the gun. In the 1930s, after sport hunters protested the decline of this game bird, many states trapped and transferred thousands of turkeys from plentiful to

wild turkey

scarce areas, successfully restoring them to much of their former range.

The wild turkey is long, lean, and slender compared to its domestic cousin, which is bred to be short, heavy, and stocky. Although a male wild turkey weighs up to twenty pounds, it can get off the ground quickly if flushed and can fly up to fifty-five miles an hour.

You can distinguish a tom, or gobbler (male), from a hen (female) by its color and characteristics. The breast feathers of hens are lighter and tipped with brown; gobbler feathers are darker and edged in black. Each has a distinctive iridescence to its plumage that makes it shine with bronze, green, brown, blue, red, or purple colors, depending on how the sunlight strikes it.

The gobbler has other impressive appendages. A fleshy growth called the "wattles" hangs beneath its chin. Another growth known as a "caruncle" protrudes from its neck. A "snood" of skin drapes over its bill. A gobbler has a sharp, bony spear on the back of each leg that it uses in fighting. Its head serves as a barometer of its emotional state: it is bright red when the gobbler unfurls all feathers to strut during the mating season, but turns blue when the bird is frightened.

To find food, a turkey scratches the ground with its feet, kicking leaves and duff behind as it claws and pecks. It ranges several miles a day. In spring it concentrates on tender greens, leftover nuts, and early insects. In summer it seeks insects, fruits, seeds, roots, and buds, while the fall brings acorns, fruit, and other seeds. In winter, when food is sparse, it looks for a seep where groundwater emerges along a hillside, nourishing fresh vegetation as food.

The turkey is a gregarious bird. Each evening it flies into a tree to roost with a group of six to forty other birds. In early morning it flutters to the ground and emits a *cluck-cluck* call to others to regroup for the day's feeding.

Other distinctive turkey sounds include a whistlelike *kee-kee-run* made by a young bird and the *ill-obble-obble-obble* sound made by the gobbler in the spring when it wants to attract a hen. Some sporting goods stores carry calls you can blow through to duplicate turkey sounds, perhaps attracting the birds to come your way.

Wild turkeys, the largest of the upland game birds, are shy and have excellent hearing and eyesight. They are related to other chickenlike wild birds such as grouse, quail, and pheasant.

Woodchuck

Glancing across the meadow I saw something that looked like a small brown stump. I focused my binoculars on the object just in time to see a twitch of its head.

woodchuck

It was a woodchuck, sitting ramrod stiff atop its burrow entrance in the Cades Cove area of Great Smoky Mountains National Park, its eyes, ears, and nose alert to any danger.

Like a sentry it sat, reminding me of marmots in the Rocky Mountains and prairie dogs of the Great Plains. All are members of the same family, as are the smaller ground squirrel and chipmunk.

A muscular body, short powerful legs, and sturdy claws make the woodchuck (also known as a groundhog) an excellent digger. It excavates burrows three to six feet below the ground. As its sharp front claws dig, its hindfeet scrape the loose dirt out behind the animal.

The burrow descends at a sharp angle below the entry hole, then levels off into a narrower tunnel that may meander as far as forty-five feet. The woodchuck will often dig one or more side tunnels that provide two or three back entrances. These "drop holes" are inconspicuous, lacking the obvious pile of dirt that defines the main entrance. The woodchuck uses these back doors as lookouts or to dive underground in a hurry when surprised by a predator like a fox.

A woodchuck is relatively easy to spot in an open meadow because of its size. About two feet long, the size of a small dog, it can weigh ten pounds or more. Woodchucks are heaviest following the summer, when they eat ravenously to put on the layer of fat that sees them through their long winter hibernation.

This hungry rodent generally does not move far to find food because it eats such a variety of vegetation, including green grasses, weed shoots, clover, and dandelion greens. If a farm is nearby, the woodchuck is only too happy to munch a farmer's beans, peas, carrots, alfalfa, or corn.

Woodchucks do not seem to require much drinking water; they often live far from streams, lakes, or creeks. Like rabbits, they get moisture from succulent plants, dew, and water left standing after a rainfall.

Woodchucks are usually solitary—they're not sociable animals except for a mother and her dependent youngsters. Most live alone in a burrow, and the burrows are widely scattered to allow each animal enough territory for foraging. But the woodchuck burrow is such a splendid storm cellar that occasionally an uninvited guest, such as a quail or a pheasant, drops in to find refuge.

Chipmunk

The chipmunk is the answer to a wildlife watcher's dream: it is active during daylight hours, easily visible, and fun to watch. Hike any forest trail or stroll the paths of a park, refuge, or national forest and you're likely to see this scampering rodent.

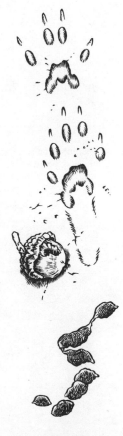

chipmunk

On warm sunny days we saw numerous chipmunks searching for food scraps near visitor centers—to the delight of amused onlookers. They hop in one direction, pick up a nut in sharp teeth, sit upright to test the quality of their discoveries, tuck a good nut into bulging cheek pouches, and dart away to burrows—all the while emitting high-pitched *chip-chip-chip* sounds to warn other chipmunks away from their territories.

Look for chipmunks in open deciduous woods that have plenty of stumps and logs, along forest edges, in fence rows between farm fields, under barns and buildings—even in city parks and suburban gardens. The chipmunk has adapted to living close to people—but just out of their reach.

The chipmunk is a member of the family that includes squirrels, ground squirrels, marmots, and woodchucks. Like a squirrel, it sports a large, furry tail. Unlike a squirrel, it has distinctive "racing stripes"—five black and two white stripes—that run the length of its six-inch brown body and arc across its head.

The Eastern Chipmunk is common throughout most of the East, Midwest, and South. Its cousins are found in the West. Of twenty-one western species, the Least Chipmunk is the most widespread, populating most of the West's mountain region.

Take a look at a chipmunk's feet. Each hindfoot has five clawed toes for good traction. Each forefoot has four clawed toes and a fifth thumblike digit with a soft rounded nail that helps the little rodent handle its food.

A Least Chipmunk at Yellowstone National Park discovers three grapes left by a picnicker. Chipmunks and ground squirrels are common and easily seen at many national parks and wildlife refuges, but are quick to dart for their burrows if startled.

A chipmunk's home and underground castle is the burrow it uses for several years. Each year the burrow grows in complexity and length—up to a total of thirty feet—as the chipmunk excavates branching tunnels, alternate exits, and extra chambers. The resident removes the excavated dirt in its cheek pouches, discarding it far from the main entrance, which it carefully camouflages among leaves and rocks. Somewhere in this underground home the chipmunk builds a foot-square nesting chamber lined with leaves and grass.

To prepare for winter, the chipmunk plugs its burrow entrances to seal out cold and keep out predators, which include coyotes, weasels, snakes, and foxes. It then makes a nest of leaves atop its food hoard and curls up for a long sleep. But unlike its fat marmot cousins, which hibernate straight through the cold months, the trim four-ounce chipmunk often wakes up hungry and has to reach down under its bed to pull out a snack.

When outside its burrow the chipmunk must be wary of other predators such as hawks, owls, and bobcats as it darts about. Its diet includes seeds, nuts, mushrooms, berries, corn, and fruits as well as bird's eggs, insects, snails, earthworns, millipedes, salamanders, and even small snakes and frogs. The busy rodent either eats its meal on the spot or carries it back to its burrow to stash away for the winter.

Squirrels

As you become acquainted with various species of tree squirrels you'll find that each of them shares a badge of glory—its handsome bushy tail. A squirrel's tail serves it well. It is a stabilizer when the squirrel leaps from branch to branch, a parachute when the animal makes a misstep and drops to the ground, an umbrella in the rain, and a blanket in the cold.

The three varieties of tree squirrels that inhabit Eastern woodlands—the red, gray, and fox squirrels—vary in size, color, and habitat, but share other traits. The fox squirrel, the largest of the three (one to three pounds), is rust with a yellowish belly. The gray squirrel (¾ to 1½ pounds) has a gray coat. The red squirrel (the smallest at ¾ pounds) is also the noisiest; it is reddish and inhabits both the Northeast and the Rocky Mountain West. All are energetic food gatherers. In one week a squirrel consumes as much as 1½ pounds of nuts, berries, seeds, flowers, insects, and mushrooms—some of which are poisonous to man.

When it finds a nut, the squirrel picks it up with its front paws, sits back on its haunches, and turns the nut over to test its soundness. If it is cracked, the squirrel eats it on the spot. Even a hard nut presents little problem to a squirrel. Its lower incisor teeth can pierce and crack a hard shell and dig out the tender kernel inside.

fox squirrel

If the nut is whole, it is set aside to be enjoyed later. The squirrel digs a hole in the ground with its front paws, then forces the nut into the hole, pointed end downward. It quickly scratches dirt over the buried nut, patting it down tightly. Nearby leaves and grass are brushed over the hole to camouflage. Later the squirrel uses its acute sense of smell to find most of these buried nuts—the ones it doesn't find will grow into trees!

As you walk the trails, keep your eyes open for two types of squirrel nests that accommodate the two litters the female squirrel usually produces each year. The female squirrel builds a winter nest in a tree cavity where her February offspring will be protected from the weather. Later she builds a second nest of leaves high in a tree to raise her summer litter, usually born in August.

Squirrels are up and about hunting for food during daylight hours. Watch for them running in delayed dashes across the forest floor and up the nearest tree trunk with food for the family. And listen for the *cut-cut-cut* or *chir-r-r-r* warning calls they make to alert other squirrels that you have invaded their domain. They sound the same warning for a marauding owl or bobcat.

One other species, the flying squirrel, inhabits forests of the East, Central, and Western states—though you will be lucky to see one. Flying squirrels forage for an hour or two before sunrise and two hours after dark. Membranes that stretch between its limbs and a flattened tail enable this squirrel to glide effortlessly between trees to search for food and to escape its enemies.

Mouse, Rat, Vole, Lemming, Shrew, and Mole

These little animals, rangers will tell you, may not be the most thrilling wildlife you will see, but they are among the most vital to the maintenance of the balance of nature in the animal world.

They seek protection by foraging at night and by burrowing underground; nevertheless these rodents sustain a high casualty rate. They provide the main food source for meat eaters such as foxes, coyotes, owls, eagles, hawks, mountain lions, bobcats, and weasels. As a consequence, most have short lives; but nature compensates by providing them with numerous litters.

Several hundred different species make up these families, which function as clean-up crews of the forests, grasslands, mountains, and deserts.

A number of species of mice inhabit every sort of terrain. Mice eat almost anything they can find: seeds, nuts, berries, insects, worms, spiders, bird's eggs, even dead mice. What they don't eat they carry in cheek pouches and tuck away in grass-lined nests. Mice commonly build their nests in hollow logs, tree stumps, or root cavities, but some attach a snug nest to a stalk of

white-footed mouse

high grass or even build a nest high in a tree.

A rat is larger than a mouse and has a long tail. It has large eyes and ears and long sensitive whiskers that equip it for nocturnal life. Rats are attracted to shiny objects—they will drop whatever they are carrying to pick up something shiny to take back to their nests.

The little vole, which looks like the familiar domesticated hamster, has brown fur, a short tail, and a blunter nose than the mouse or rat. Look under a log or in tree roots for a vole's nest, woven from grass, leaves, or moss. It is active year-round—more often in darkness but sometimes during daylight—and follows well-worn runways in the grass or leafy forest floor. It gets its name from a Scandinavian word meaning "meadow."

The lemming is about five inches long and has much the same appearance as the vole, its eyes, ears, feet, and short tail almost hidden by its long soft fur. It scurries about both night and day, munching succulent grasses. It digs short underground tunnels with side chambers for resting, feeding, and storing food. Grass clippings line its runways and flank the entrance to its feeding stations. Every year female lemmings produce two or three litters, each containing as many as eight young.

The shrew, which is the size of a mouse, is a carnivore (meat eater). It is the only mammal definitely known to have a poisonous bite. A voracious eater, it gobbles up in a day its own weight in insects and other small prey, including mice. Its runways form crooked pathways over the ground or beneath grass and leaves. Although it is vulnerable to larger animals, the shrew gives off a musky smell that makes it highly distasteful to some predators.

Moles spend most of their lives beneath the ground, emerging only occasionally. Highly adapted for digging, moles have powerful shoulder muscles and broad forefeet armed with long, flattened claws that pull their cylindrical bodies through underground tunnels in search of earthworms, insects, and grubs. Though you may never see the mole, you will find it easy to spot its tunnels, which push the ground's surface up about an inch, leaving a raised pattern in a field or meadow. When a mole enlarges its underground living quarters it carries soil to the end of a tunnel, pushing the dirt out onto the surface where it becomes a molehill.

Hawks

The undisputed enemy of ground-dwelling rodents like the squirrel, chipmunk, and mouse, hawks strike like feathered lightning from the sky.

With powerful wings, streamlined bodies, sharp eyesight, and curved talons that can seize and crush prey, hawks belong to a large family of birds of prey called raptors.

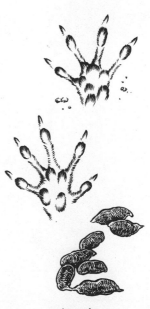

wood rat

pine vole

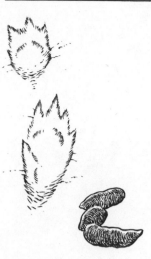

lemming

short-tailed shrew

Laurie Goodrich, a staff biologist at the Hawk Mountain Sanctuary located atop a ridge in eastern Pennsylvania's Appalachian Mountains, provided Marge and me a firsthand insight into these birds on a gray October day at the height of the fall migration season.

We joined her at a rocky promontory overlooking the parallel ridges and valleys that form part of the Atlantic flyway. The flyway is one of four aerial routes that span the United States from north to south, along which birds migrate from chill temperatures and dwindling food supplies of the North to the warmer climates of Florida and Central and South America.

We walked out over a jumble of huge sandstone boulders to a rough stone cockpit, a command post for the staff biologist who keeps the sanctuary's official bird count for the day. Before her stood a compact spotting scope on a tripod. A clipboard for recording hourly counts lay on a flat rock. Laurie wore a pair of binoculars around her neck, and tucked in a nearby crevice was a walkie-talkie for contact with the sanctuary visitor center.

Not only did Laurie keep count of the birds that passed her observation point, she also provided an informative running commentary on the dynamics of hawk migration for the visitors gathered around her.

"There's a bird over Little Pinnacle," she announced, loud enough so that all of us standing or sitting on the rocks could hear.

"Looks like a red-tailed hawk," she added, pointing toward one of the mountain landmarks observers use to locate the approaching birds.

"Put the bottom of your binocular field on the tree line at the top of Little Pinnacle," she said, indicating a ridge four miles to the north of us. "Now you should have the hawk in your field of vision."

"I got it," came the responses from bird watchers. We watched as the red-tail glided along the ridgeline, buoyed by an updraft created by wind deflected up the mountainside. Laurie explained that the red-tailed hawk is a buteo, one of the four classes of hawks, a type that has broad wings.

"Bird over Number One," Laurie sang out a few moments later. (Number One is one of five other recognizable points along the ridgeline.) Binoculars swung to pick up the speck in the sky two miles away.

Laurie kept her binoculars at her eyes, at the same time offering further clues to the new bird's identity. "It's in the falcon class, smaller than a buteo. See the narrow pointed wings and the longer tail? It's slim, built to dive." Finally the clincher: "It's a merlin," she concluded, as the bird swept over the ridge and disappeared from sight.

Later we saw more red-tailed hawks circling over the valley. Laurie noted that these birds were "kettling," or circling and rising on a column of warm air known as a "thermal." When the thermal dissipates, the hawks drift

The red-tailed hawk is one of many raptor species and other birds that migrate along north-south flyways that span North America. Shenandoah Seasonal Ranger Rick Potvin holds a tethered red-tail that observers usually see high in the sky.

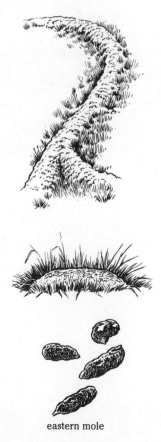

downridge to find another thermal or an updraft. By floating on these thermals, the birds save the energy required to constantly flap their wings. She added that sailplane pilots, like birds, seek updrafts and thermals to gain altitude.

During our watch on the mountaintop we were joined by some seventy other observers, all eager to see the fall migration. These were but a handful of the forty-eight thousand people who visit this popular sanctuary every year.

A teacher appeared with his high school class from nearby Kutztown. A woman who had worked the early shift at her job came to spend the afternoon scanning the sky. A local housewife, a regular observer at Hawk Mountain, participated in the animated conversation between bird sightings. Barry Peifer, a veteran on the mountaintop, took the day off from his job and willingly helped Laurie with bird identifications and coaching the newcomers. Hawk watching, it seems, is not a solitary event, but a social one.

Back at the visitor center, Jim Brett, curator of the sanctuary, recalled the biggest day in the history of Hawk Mountain.

"September 14, 1978, was exceptional," Jim remembered. "The East was under the influence of a massive cold front pushing down from Canada. By 8 A.M. more

eastern mole

red-tailed hawk

than five hundred broadwings had been seen rising out of the forest. They were joining larger groups moving across the ridge from the northeast.

"The hawks were coming in a huge band up to a mile wide. And come they did," he smiled. "By 11 A.M. we were overwhelmed. Birds were everywhere, as far to the north as our binoculars could see.

"Kettles of broadwings usually contain several hundred birds; we were trying to count kettles of more than a thousand. Between 11 A.M. and noon, thirty-five hundred hawks were recorded. An incredible eighty-five hundred broadwings passed overhead between noon and 1 P.M. After the full eight-hour day we had recorded 21,448 broadwings!"

If you decide to visit a good hawk-watching site along the Atlantic, Mississippi River, Rocky Mountain, or Pacific Coast flyways, Jim Brett has some advice for you.

Bring a good pair of binoculars or a spotting scope, he counsels, and wear warm clothing. Sitting for six or more hours on a windswept mountain in fall or spring can be chilly.

Experienced hawk watchers also carry plenty of food and several thermoses of hot tea or coffee. A hat to protect against wind or sun, insect repellent, sunscreen lotion, a blanket, and a cushion or chair can also come in handy. Temperatures often rise or fall in these exposed locations by thirty degrees or more between early morning and afternoon.

Plan to come in a group. Extra pairs of eyes are useful and it will be fun to share your hawk-watching adventure with others.

Bald Eagle

Come November and December, wildlife enthusiasts, bird watchers, and school biology teachers in Pennsylvania and Maryland know just where to go to get a good view of the nation's symbol, the bald eagle.

They head for the Conowingo Dam on the Susquehanna River where plentiful gizzard shad and the turbulence of water surging through the dam combine to produce a perfect bald eagle feeding ground.

Many migrating eagles stop and snag fish at Conowingo on their way south along the Atlantic flyway. A few have even set up winter housekeeping nearby. One pair has a nest on a farm near the two and a half miles of shoreline that the Philadelphia Electric Company, the dam's operator, has set aside as protected roosting area for these winter visitors. Three other pairs of eagles have established nests a little farther downriver within the U.S. Army's Aberdeen Proving Ground.

Up to a hundred and fifty people a day come to see the eagles. As they watch, the big birds circle over the river, diving down to snatch the luckless shad from the water with their talons. One eagle perched on a tall transmission tower for such a long time that Charlotte Ault, a staff naturalist employed by the company, joked that "the visitors must have thought we had the bird under contract!"

The bald eagle is truly an all-American bird—the only species of eagle unique to our continent. When our ancestors gave this handsome bird its name, "bald" meant "white-headed," not "hairless" as it does today. Back then, it soared over most of what is now the continental United States, but today the only great assemblage is an estimated fifty thousand birds in Alaska.

The bald eagle is listed as "endangered" in forty-three of the forty-eight contiguous states and "threatened" in the remaining five. It finds its prime nesting areas along the rivers and coast of the Middle Atlantic states, in Florida, in the upper reaches of Minnesota and Michigan, and in wilderness areas of the mountainous West, where its relative the golden eagle also lives.

With its majestic proportions, the bald eagle is one of nature's most imposing birds of prey. Males generally measure almost three feet from head to tail, weigh eight to ten pounds, and spread their wings about six and a half feet. Females are even larger, with lengths of three and a half feet, weights up to fourteen pounds, and wingspans of eight feet. The bird's chocolate brown body and huge, pale eyes, fierce yellow beak, and grasping, black talons add to its formidability. Its distinctive white head and tail feathers appear only after the bird is four to five years old, replacing a mottled brown coloring.

The bald eagle is basically a fish eater, swooping from above to snatch its prey from the water's surface or wading into the shallows along the shore. Eagles can be intimidating. They have been known to intercept an osprey, harass it until it drops a fish it has caught, and then seize the falling fish in midair and carry it back to their nests.

Bald eagles have few natural enemies. But they require a special kind of environment—relative isolation and tall, mature trees or cliffs in which to build their huge nests. Eagle nests are usually five to six feet across, fashioned with sticks and grass. Unless they are disturbed, eagles return to the same nest year after year, improving it with each use.

Concerns about whether our national symbol can survive have now eased. In earlier days the cutting of forests for lumber and farms eliminated much eagle habitat. The use of agricultural pesticides caused eagles to lay such thin-shelled eggs that they broke in the nest, taking a heavy toll until DDT and other chemicals were banned in the 1970s. Now biologists believe that the bald eagle is making a comeback, offering wildlife watchers more opportunities to see this magnificent bird.

bald eagle

CHAPTER 6

Wildlife of the Pines and Marshes

All was quiet when we first arrived at the pond in Everglades National Park. We could barely see each other in the predawn darkness of the February morning. As the first gray of dawn diluted the blackness, we heard an occasional splash when a bird stepped into water, the *bar-rumpf* of a bullfrog, and an assortment of high-pitched calls of wading birds as they aroused themselves for a new day.

As daylight brightened the scene we made out a great white heron at the pond edge preening its feathers. A white wood stork stood on one foot surveying the situation. An egret flew to a low overhanging branch where it could get a better look at the fish in the pond, now revealed in the growing light. Other herons stalked the shallows and several species of ducks circled the pond searching for breakfast.

Rangers at the park's visitor center had recommended the dawn hour at the pond as the best time to see a variety of wading birds. Winter, the dry season at Everglades, finds birds and other wildlife clustered at ponds. It was quite a show: the birds stalking at the pond's edge, stirring the water with their feet, then thrusting their beaks into the water to gobble a fish or a snail. As a bird captured its prey, it flew off to try another feeding area.

Much of the wildlife in the southern part of the United States—like the bird life at Everglades—lives in or near water. Streams bordered with high grass and aquatic plants meander to the sea. Marshes and swamps are abundant along the fringe of coastal land that sweeps from Virginia through the Carolinas, Georgia, Florida, Alabama, Mississippi, and Louisiana into Texas. High temperatures, ample rainfall, sandy soil, and a long growing season characterize the region.

Cypress trees spread their extensive root systems into the water; curious growths called "knees" surround their trunks. Mangroves grow away from tidal shores, forming new islands that provide nesting areas for birds. Marsh-loving animals such as beaver, opossum, and raccoon thrive in the watery environment, as do amphibians, fish-eating birds, and a record number of snakes.

At the southern tip of this coastal zone lies the Everglades, the only subtropical wilderness area in the United States. Water from Lake Okeechobee flows southward across this flat terrain into the Gulf of Mexico. The sea of sawgrass is dotted with patches of open water and islands of vegetation called hammocks. The hammocks support tropical trees such as palms, gumbo-limbo, and mahogany, as well as ferns, orchids, and a variety of epiphytes, or air-breathing plants. In this watery world live the only crocodilians in the United States—the alligator and the American crocodile.

The southern lowlands, or piedmont, lie inland from the coast. Here grow slash, long-leaf, and loblolly pine, producing pine forests where sunlight is more abundant than it is in the leafy forests of the Eastern woodlands. White-tailed deer, squirrels, rabbits, turkeys, and skunks thrive in the piney woods.

Farther inland the land slopes upward into the southern section of the Appalachian Mountains. Ridges and valleys in this mountainous zone are covered with deciduous trees such as post oak, hickory, and holly, suitable habitat for deer and black bear.

Alligator

The alligator was once a common sight in lakes, swamps, and rivers along the Gulf of Mexico and up the Atlantic coast as far north as North Carolina—even making its way a considerable distance up the Mississippi River. But hunters killed these amphibious reptiles by the thousands, sending their leathery hides to market to make fashionable alligator shoes, wallets, and handbags. Swamps were filled in or drained for development, shrinking the alligator's habitat.

By the 1960s the alligator seemed in danger of vanishing. In 1967 the U.S. Fish and Wildlife Service designated the animal as an endangered species and called on state governments to make it unlawful to hunt the alligator.

I had the opportunity in the 1960s to witness the efforts of the state of Florida to intercept poachers who continued to hunt and kill alligators. One day I accompanied ranger Windle "Clem" Clemons, of the Florida Game and Fresh Water Fish Commission, on an airboat patrol of the sawgrass wilderness north of Everglades National Park to learn how poachers evaded the law.

alligator

Clem explained that lawbreakers hunted alligators under cover of darkness; they used a powerful light that hypnotized the animal. An alternate method used a large, baited hook to snag and hold a hungry alligator.

Toward the end of the day's patrol we saw evidence of a poacher's work. A dead alligator lay sprawled in the shallows, probably shot and left behind by a lawbreaker fearful of being caught before he could remove the carcass.

Today the alligator has a brighter future for several reasons. Many customers have been educated about the animal's plight and refuse to buy merchandise made from natural alligator hide. Synthetic materials have been developed to take the place of the real thing. Tough state hunting laws protecting alligators have been enacted and enforced.

Rangers at Everglades explain that Florida's alligator population increased so rapidly that in 1977 the Secretary of the Interior downgraded the designation of the alligator from endangered to "threatened," and again in 1987 to "biologically secure."

Marge and I were gratified to see a number of alligators on the February day we walked the Anhinga Trail at the Everglades. The trail is named for the remarkable bird that dives beneath the water for its prey. A raised boardwalk and pathway circles the sawgrass marshland, leading visitors past alligators, softshelled turtles, fish, anhingas, blue herons, green herons, gallinules, egrets, and other wading birds.

Wildlife observers get a good view of alligators sunning themselves on a mudbank or log or lying almost submerged with only eyes and snout above water. Alligators themselves seem little disturbed by a crowd of peering faces.

Before walking the trail, we listened to a ranger talk and learned that the modern alligator is the product of a long evolution. It is a descendent of the cold-blooded reptiles that roamed the earth during the Age of Reptiles 140 million years ago.

Far from the fearsome dragon that myths made it out to be, the alligator is a shy creature. Its name is derived from *el legarto*, the lizard, coined by early Spaniards.

The park staff cannot recall any alligator attacks on humans. For the most part this creature eats fish, snakes, frogs, turtles, and small animals that it catches in or near the water. Flaps over its ears and a special respiratory system enable it to eat while submerged without breathing water into its lungs.

Usually dull gray in color, alligators are most at home in water. They propel themselves by waving their tails from side to side.

On the prowl for prey, an alligator lies deceptively still in the water, eyes alert. When a fish swims by, its huge mouth opens, then snaps shut with a force of up to twelve hundred pounds per square inch. Surprisingly, the big animal eats only once or twice a week. The rest of its time is spent basking in warm sun or lying in mud caves.

In the Everglades, the rangers told us, the alligator plays an important role in maintaining the balance of nature. One of its favorite foods is the bony garfish, a fish that has few enemies in the fish world. If the alligator did not consume numerous garfish, the gars would deplete the Everglades of such other fish as bass and bream.

Visitors to South Florida or Louisiana during the spring mating season might hear the throaty bellow of the male alligator seeking to attract a mate and proclaim its territory. After mating, the female, carrying vegetation in its teeth, builds a large nest, hollowing out its middle by kicking at it. In the dish-shaped center she lays thirty to seventy eggs. She covers them with soil, grass, and leaves to protect them from marauding otters, raccoons, herons, and snapping turtles, then submerges in water nearby, close enough to keep an eye on her nest.

The heat created by the decomposition of the vegetation promotes the development of the eggs, which hatch in about nine weeks. When the mother alligator hears an impatient *rumpf rumpf* noise coming from the eggs, she kicks away the covering layer to expose the eggs. Baby alligators puncture their shells and break through them to be born. Sometimes the female carries an egg in her mouth to the water's edge so that the baby can more readily make its way to water after emerging. Hatchlings are only eight inches long and weigh two ounces, a tiny beginning for what will someday be a huge alligator.

Alligators grow a little more than a foot a year. Both males and females mature when they're about five years old and six feet long. From then on the male grows faster. At full growth the male may reach twelve feet, the female eight.

Alligators in the Everglades and similar environments have an important role to play in times of drought. When the prairielike expanse of the Everglades, a "river of grass," runs dry, the alligator wriggles its body and sweeps its tail from side to side, eventually building up the land around it to excavate a "gator hole."

As the rest of the glades dry out, the gator hole provides a reservoir of water where fish, amphibians, turtles, and other invertebrates take refuge. Were it not for the gator holes, many of these animals would suffocate in the hot mud. Birds, deer, raccoons, and other creatures survive in drought times by drawing on the gator hole for their water supply.

Crocodile

Crocodiles, now rare in the United States, probably live only in the Everglades, in nearby Biscayne Bay, and along the Florida Keys. Whereas alligators prefer a fresh

crocodile

water habitat, the crocodile lives in salt water.

The two are easy to distinguish, even though at first glance they appear similar. The crocodile is olive green, the alligator dull gray. The crocodile's snout tapers to a point; the alligator's is blunt shaped. The alligator's teeth fit closely together when it closes its mouth. But a crocodile's bite leaves one large tooth on each side of its lower jaw protruding prominently outside its mouth.

At last report, biologists knew of only eighteen crocodile nests anywhere in the United States, making this amphibian one of our most endangered species.

Manatee

The manatee, an ungainly marine mammal found along the coasts of Florida, is often called a "sea cow." For good reason. Like a cow, it grazes on vegetation for up to eight hours each day, feeding on a variety of sea plants that grow in shoal water.

Like the crocodile, the manatee is listed as one of this country's endangered animals. Although it once flourished from North Carolina to the Texas coast, the manatee was hunted to near extinction around the turn of the century. Commercial hunters slaughtered the docile animal for its oil, hide, and meat, which they advertised as "sea beefsteaks."

Blimplike manatees nuzzle each other in the warm waters of Florida's Crystal River. **Photo by Fred Bavendam.**

Today the best places to see one is at four national wildlife refuges in Florida: Hobe Sound and Merritt Island on Florida's east coast and Crystal River and Ding Darling on the state's west coast.

These blimplike seagoing animals have a large flat tail, two front flippers shaped like paddles, and a relatively small head. They range in color from slate gray to brown and are sometimes marked with pinkish scars or scrapes. Their true color may be obscured by a covering of algae or barnacles, a result of its long submersion in the water.

The manatee spends two-thirds of the year in coastal lagoons. From mid-November to March, when lagoon temperatures cool, these rotund swimmers head for warmer coastal sanctuaries. They migrate up several of Florida's rivers fed by springs that keep the water temperature near seventy degrees Fahrenheit. Biologists estimate that altogether about twelve hundred manatees spend the winter in Florida waters.

The manatee grows to lengths of eight to twelve feet and may weigh a thousand pounds or more. To fill its big frame it must eat about one-quarter of its weight each day, a formidable amount. Feeding mostly at night, consumes bottom vegetation such as eelgrass, seagrass, water hyacinths, alligator weed, and marine algae. It usually grazes in shallows but occasionally hauls its bulk up on riverbanks to munch on waterside vegetation.

This remarkable creature is the only herbivorous mammal that spends its entire life in water. As a mammal, of course, it must breathe, but the manatee can remain submerged for ten to fifteen minutes before it must propel itself to the surface with several sweeps of its tail to replenish its air supply. Breathing occurs through its snout, allowing the animal to stay well hidden under water. Its muscular lungs compress stored air, making it easier to hold a breath. Its dense bone structure provides the ballast to neutralize its buoyancy while underwater. Manatees can even go to sleep underwater for brief periods before having to surface for another break.

Several manatees may swim together in a small, loosely associated herd. In winter, groups of twenty or more may gather together around a warm spring. They nuzzle, cavort, and seem to enjoy each other's company. Some manatees have lived thirty years in captivity; biologists estimate that they may live as long as fifty years in the wild.

In Tampa Bay, some eighty manatees a year have been sliced to death by speedboat propellers. As a consequence, save-the-manatee clubs have been organized by conservationists to educate boaters to stay away from manatees.

The U.S. Fish and Wildlife Service operates a boat in King's Bay in the Crystal River National Wildlife Refuge. Here, wildlife specialists inform visitors about the manatee and help protect these unusual mammals from swimmers, boaters, and divers.

As many as forty thousand divers come to King's Bay every winter to see the manatees, who do not seem to mind the visitors. The animals often nudge and nuzzle each other. Divers may swim along with the manatees and even pet them, but rules dictate that a diver should not touch a manatee unless the mammal makes the first approach.

Opossum

opossum

You might chance upon an opossum some night while driving along a dark road through a forested area. Watch for the dull orange shine of its eyes in your headlights and the outline of an animal about the size of a cat. This nighttime prowler has grayish white hair, large hairless ears that protrude from its head, and a narrow face covered with white hair and tapering to a pointed snout.

Early French explorers called it a *rat de bois*, "rat of the woods," because of the opossum's long tail. The tail serves as a sort of fifth hand. When the opossum climbs a tree in search of food it uses its tail to steady its body on a tree limb or even to suspend itself while it snags a piece of fruit or escapes from a predator. Favorite foods include fruits, vegetables, nuts, berries, bird's eggs, beetles, grasshoppers, earthworms, and mice.

The opossum's major claim to fame comes not from its long tail but from the way the female opossum raises her young. The opossum is the only marsupial—an animal that carries its young in a pouch that forms a built-in incubator on its belly—in the United States.

Up to fourteen tiny opossums are born in each litter. The babies are so small that the entire litter fits in a teaspoon. The newborns crawl up the mother's stomach to the pouch where they nurse and grow for two months. Then they emerge, clinging to their mother's back. The young opossums soon begin to forage on their own but continue to hitch a ride with their mother until they become fully independent at three to four months of age. In the mild temperatures of the Southeast, female opossums usually produce two such litters each year.

The opossum looks ferocious with its narrow snout and fifty teeth but it is really quite timid. As a night hunter its keen sense of hearing is its best hunting weapon. Its ears twitch as it listens for any noise that will give away the exact location of its prey.

If preyed upon, the opossum uses a unique defense: it feigns death, actually seeming to fall into a trance with its eyes and mouth open, its body completely limp. At the same time, it exudes a smell repellent to other animals. If a predator is fooled and departs, the opossum quickly recovers and walks away.

The solitary opossum may prowl a mile or more at night on a foraging patrol. After a meal, it sits on its hind legs and tail and washes itself like a cat. It does not hibernate in cold weather but may hole up in a hollow tree, stump, or road culvert for several days. When hungry, it emerges, even in freezing temperatures, risking frostbite to its naked ears and tail.

Opossum tracks look like small human hand prints. The tracks of the hindfeet show the animal's opposable "thumb," a digit like the human thumb that enables the opossum to grasp an object firmly with its hind foot.

Raccoon

Everyone seems to have a favorite story about raccoons. One campground host watched a raccoon make a nightly round of campsites, methodically opening trash cans to sample the contents. A friend in the suburbs taps on his porch to tell the neighborhood raccoon to approach for a handout.

raccoon

The raccoon, a species found only in North America, is intelligent and adaptable, and is among the few animals that actually thrive in the face of encroaching development. It can live with man and like it—even if humans do not always welcome it. Raccoons are found in almost every state, even thriving within the limits of New York City. Biologists estimate that there are more raccoons in the United States today than when European settlers first arrived.

The animal is immediately recognizable because of its grizzled, gray brown color, the black rings that encircle its bushy tail, and the black "mask" around its eyes, which reveals this backyard bandit for what it really is.

Rangers point to two types of habitat the raccoon especially likes: streams or lakes within mixed hardwood forests and coastal marshlands. Water provides the fish, frogs, and crayfish this creature prefers, while hardwood trees offer good-sized cavities for a den and nuts and fruits to eat. Marshlands also provide a readily available supply of seafood.

A raccoon will often wade up a small stream or spring run-off searching for crayfish, aquatic insects, or minnows. Sitting on the stream bank, it will deftly sort out any crayfish and snails from among the stones. A pond backed up by a beaver dam also provides a raccoon with a good hunting habitat.

Using the long fingers on its dexterous forepaws, the raccoon can find and handle food almost as skillfully as a monkey. It feels for its prey in the shallows of a stream or in a crevice between rocks. Long sharp claws anchor slippery food items. After capturing its prey, it dunks it into the water to wash before eating. Look along stream banks for raccoon tracks that look like miniature human hand prints.

Raccoons are preyed upon by hawks, owls, bobcats, red foxes, coyotes, snakes, and alligators. With sensitive paws and long claws, it is skilled at climbing trees, which is how the raccoon escapes an enemy like a hunter's dog. On a warm, bright day you might spot a raccoon sunning itself on the limb of a tree or curled up in an abandoned squirrel nest. At night it descends to search for food, traveling, hunting, and feeding almost exclusively on the ground. It stalks at a slow amble with its head down, sniffing the ground, back arched and tail dangling, its whiskered snout and sensitive forepaws ready for instant action.

In the South, raccoons mate from January to March. Most births occur in April. An average of four young, each weighing a scant two ounces, are born after a gestation of two months. They squirm and cry to nurse from their mother; they are weaned to the adult diet in two to four months. By autumn the young raccoons weigh some fifteen pounds. They remain with their mother over the next winter, then move away to establish their own hunting territory.

A raccoon makes a variety of sounds that may help you identify it, including barks, hisses, a wailing tremolo, a contented purring sound while eating, and a piercing scream of alarm.

Muskrat

We were walking along the edge of a former beaver pond when we noticed a V-shaped wave creasing the water's smooth surface. A black nose led the way, curving into a group of lily pads, then among some cattails before swerving out into open water again.

A muskrat, said Park Ranger Sheila Willis, resembles a beaver but is only about half the size. You can tell the two apart by their tails. The beaver's tail is large and flat and it uses it like an oar. The muskrat's tail is long and narrow and it uses it like a rudder while propelling itself with its large, partially webbed feet.

The muskrat's track reflects its anatomy, she added. Between the pairs of footprints is the drag mark of the tail. The animal is reddish brown and has a luxurious coat, which made it one of the prime targets of fur traders in the early days of the West.

Like the beaver, she pointed out, the muskrat makes a lodge for its home. But unlike the beaver's dwelling, which is big and complex and made out of branches and mud, the muskrat's lodge is simpler and looks like a small haystack. With sharp teeth it cuts cattails, bulrushes, pond weeds, or other marsh vegetation, drags the material across the pond, and piles it atop a log or clump of cattails.

muskrat

After piling up a cone-shaped mound, the muskrat dives into the water and burrows up from below. With its teeth it carves out a living chamber within the mound, as well as an escape tunnel into the water. Muskrats that live along a creek or stream excavate their burrows into the soil of the stream bank, providing another escape tunnel that leads out below water.

Look for muskrat families in a marsh, estuary, lake, or pond where there are plentiful cattails and grasses, where the water is shallow enough to support water plants yet deep enough that it does not freeze to the bottom in the winter. This is important because muskrats do not store food to eat in winter and need to slip out under ice to forage for roots and stems. Their normal diet includes clams, fish, salamanders, and snails, in addition to pond vegetation.

In winter in the North you might see ice-covered ponds where several conical mounds protrude as much as two feet above the surface. These are muskrat lodges protecting their residents from the elements while they subsist comfortably beneath the ice.

This aquatic animal can dive and remain underwater for up to fifteen minutes while searching for food or escaping predators such as the mink. It is well adapted to its environment. Folds of cheek skin within its mouth form a perfect seal behind its teeth, preventing water from entering its mouth while it feeds underwater. And when it climbs out of the water, moisture runs easily off its thick, oily coat, leaving the muskrat almost dry.

You might see a muskrat at any time of day but this creature is most active at night, in the early evening, or on cool, rainy days. If its food source is too far from its home to be carried back, it will build a feeding platform of discarded vegetation at a midpoint in its foraging trip.

The species gets its name from the musk glands at the base of its tail, glands it uses to add scent to its lodge, feeding platforms, and trails through the marsh—and to attract a mate. Individuals use their distinctive odor to identify each other and to stake out their territory. Most muskrats spend their entire lives within one hundred yards of their homes, unless the water level changes and they are forced to wander farther afield in search of food or to build a new lodge.

Otter

Ask a ranger at any park or refuge that contains a watery environment whether there are otters in the park. If there are, ask if there's an otter slide. If the local otters have such a favorite sliding place, and if you can find a hidden spot to observe the activity, you could be in for one of the highlights of any wildlife-watching adventure.

The river otter is renowned for its playfulness and

otter

curiosity. Otters romp with each other or play by themselves, both as juveniles and as adults. They will slide down an embankment, making a resounding slap as they hit the water. As a family group they even take turns, like kids at a playground, slithering down a riverbank one after the other.

Other otter games involve pushing a floating stick around with the nose, dropping and retrieving pebbles in a pond, and romping in shallow water. Otters at play make a variety of sounds as they communicate with each other: chirps, chittering noises, low chucklings, and grumblings.

It's not all fun and games, however. The otter is magnificently adapted to its marine environment and to the serious business of catching its dinner.

It is a fast, graceful swimmer, probably the most adept of all the mammals. It can attain an underwater speed of seven miles an hour, swim a quarter-mile underwater without surfacing for air, and dive to a depth of fifty feet. It moves by flexing its strong, streamlined body up and down while using its feet and long tail for steering.

When searching for prey it cruises slowly, paddling with all four webbed feet. It can swim right side up, upside down, on its side, or spiraling through the water. Valvelike structures seal its ears and nose to prevent them from becoming waterlogged. Touch-sensitive whiskers help locate prey and aid in navigation by feeling along the river bottom and walls of the riverbank burrow.

The river otter's streamlined body, short legs, and webbed feet enable it to swim at speeds up to seven miles an hour.

The otter's favorite prey are minnows, sunfish, suckers, carp, and trout. Other targets are frogs, turtles, snails, mussels (it can crunch an entire mussel shell with its strong teeth), crayfish, snakes, worms, insects, aquatic plants, and roots.

The playful otter is also a restless wanderer. Although it moves awkwardly on land, it sometimes is compelled to migrate to another location in search of a fresh hunting ground or a new riverbank site for a den. With snow on the ground, however, the fun begins. The otter takes a bound, then slides ahead on its stomach. A hill becomes an otter toboggan slide.

Otters have a dark brown, glossy coat. Two layers of fur keep it warm. Long guard hairs cover a short, dense underfur. Beneath these two layers of hair is a layer of fat; together the fur and fat allow the otter to spend most of its time in the water without getting too cold, even in winter.

Otters generally live a solitary life except to mate and afterwards to raise their young. The female bears her litter of two or three pups in the late winter in the safety of her riverbank den or in an abandoned beaver or muskrat lodge. After three months the mother otter has coaxed her offspring into the water. By seven months of age the youngsters are good swimmers. Soon they learn to forage for themselves and leave home to make a new life.

Owl

Owls are creatures of the night, more often heard than seen.

These fluffy birds with large eyes have long had a reputation of mystery and superstition. Perhaps because owls are active only at night, they have been feared by people.

Actually the owl's role at night is similar to that of the hawk in daylight—both are superb, specialized predators, adapted to find, catch, and kill prey quickly and efficiently.

Owls are found throughout the United States. They range in size from elf owls no larger than a sparrow to great horned and great gray owls that have wingspans of up to five feet. Other species include the screech owl, barred owl, long-eared owl, short-eared owl, saw-whet owl, and common barn owl.

All have a distinctive broad face with prominent eyes set in feathered disks, sharp curved beaks and claws, and long fluffy feathers. An owl's feathers usually cover its legs and upper toes, areas that are without plumage in most other birds.

Owl feathers are usually gray, brown, or buff— darker colors that provide better camouflage in its night-

great horned owl

time environment. The plumage is dense and soft, making the bird appear heavier than it actually is.

Extremely large retinas, which are packed with rods, or light-gathering cells, make an owl's vision fifty to one hundred times more efficient than human eyes in distinguishing small objects in poor light. An owl differentiates colors poorly but can determine distance well: it possesses binocular vision in which each eye views the same scene from a slightly different angle, producing excellent depth perception.

Its eyes are fixed in its head. That's why an owl turns its entire head to look at you. Some species can twist their heads 270 degrees, almost completely around.

Keen hearing enhances an owl's hunting skill. Beneath its feathery head, two highly developed ears hear sounds below the threshold of human hearing. Even in complete darkness an owl can catch its prey by using its sense of hearing alone.

Aerodynamics helps too. Soft leading edges of its lightweight wings and large wing surfaces allow an owl to fly and glide in complete silence. It descends in a noiseless glide and grabs its prey with strong, sharp claws.

Owls generally kill what is easiest to catch. Mice and wood rats form a major part of the large owl's diet; a smaller owl eats insects and beetles. During daylight hours the bird stays in a hollow tree or dense stand of vegetation until evening, when it hunts again.

The full-voiced call of an owl is usually sounded to define territory or look for a mate. A softer call could be a short-range communication between parent and offspring. When cornered, a frightened owl makes a hiss or clicking sound, snapping together the upper and lower parts of its bill.

If you do not see the owl itself, look for pellets at the foot of a tree where it has roosted or fed. Owls swallow a small animal whole, assimilating the flesh of the victim. Their digestive systems separate bones, fur, feathers, and other indigestible portions and forms them into pellets. The owl then regurgitates these pellets to make room for its next meal, thereby leaving a telltale sign of its roosting place (see page 47). If you find these cylindrical pellets under a tree, come back that night and you might find the owl itself perched in the same favorite spot.

Wading Birds

Look along the shores of estuaries, lakes, ponds, and streams to experience the grand assortment of wading birds that inhabit the southern regions.

Some of the largest are the great white heron and the great blue heron, both of which stand four feet tall and have a magnificent wingspan of seven feet. The great white heron lives along the coast of Florida or

great blue heron

farther south. The great blue heron, actually blue gray in color, is a strong flier and ranges throughout most of the United States and Canada. Silent and alone, the heron stalks along the shore with a stately stride in its search for food. It stands in the water, stiff as a statue, until a fish glides past its feet. As soon as it spies its prey, the heron makes a lightning stab, piercing the victim with its spear-like bill.

Another large and showy wading bird is the common egret. This long-legged inhabitant of the swamps of the Southeast is now protected in wildlife refuges in South Carolina, Florida, Louisiana, and Texas, but once was threatened by plume hunters who pursued the birds to obtain their feathery aigrettes to use in fashionable women's hats. But the big white bird is now protected and its numbers are increasing. Another egret, the snowy egret, nests in ponds, bays, or salt marshes along the Atlantic and Gulf coasts and wanders as far north as southern Canada.

Many wading birds converge on Florida's marshlands during the breeding season from November to April to lay their eggs and hatch their young.

Observers have reported colonies of up to a half-million white ibises nesting together in the Everglades. The white ibis is a striking sight. Its plumage is pure white except for shiny, blue-black wingtips. Its bill, legs and the bare flesh around its eyes are bright red. It uses its long, curved beak to snatch frogs, small fish, and snails from marshy shallows, wet fields, and tidal flats.

The roseate spoonbill, on the other hand, is easily identifiable by its pink wings and the spatular shape of its broad bill. The spoonbill obtains food in a different manner, by swinging its beak from side to side as it searches the shallows. Its gorgeous coloring almost caused the extinction of this bird, which was regularly gunned down by plume hunters. In 1939, according to conservationists, only thirty spoonbills remained in Florida. But with wildlife protection, the population increased to more than four hundred by the mid-1950s. The big pink wading bird is now no longer endangered.

Ducks

Wildlife watchers as well as hunters can enjoy the massive migrations of ducks from wintering areas to nesting grounds in the North.

Each spring and fall these hardy birds travel hundreds of miles, often in large flocks, following one of four major flyways, or flight paths. Spanning the country from north to south, these flight paths follow the Pacific coast, the Rocky Mountain range, the Mississippi River valley, and the Atlantic coast.

More than forty different kinds of ducks live on the North American continent. They are characterized by

duck

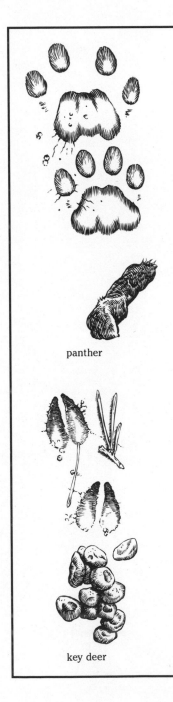

panther

key deer

Two Threatened Species

Wildlife watchers who make a special effort in Florida might be rewarded with a glimpse of two animals that remain on the endangered species list—the panther and the key deer.

The panther, a cousin of the western mountain lion, has been hunted almost to extinction. Biologists estimate that only about thirty of the graceful cats still survive, most of them in the backcountry of Big Cypress National Preserve and Everglades National Park. The panther is not black, as many believe, but tawny like its western cousin. It is carnivorous; it stalks, kills, and consumes deer, wild hogs, small mammals, and birds—even occasionally an alligator.

The Florida Game and Fresh Water Fish Commission has joined hands with the U.S. Fish and Wildlife Service, the National Park Service, and two private businesses in an effort to preserve the present population of panthers and extend the animal's range into other wilderness areas. The Florida Panther Interagency Committee plans to breed additional panthers and release them in places where they can sustain themselves in the wild.

Whereas panthers stay away from humans, key deer are readily visible. If you drive to Big Pine Key and nearby No Name Key along the Overseas Highway to Key West you'll probably see the small key deer along the road, in open grasslands or piney woods.

The threat to the key deer comes from the continuing development of these islands. In 1954 the National Key Deer Wildlife Refuge was established to preserve this small species. A fully antlered buck stands only some twenty-eight inches high at the shoulder, a tiny spotted fawn measures less than a foot. Uncontrolled hunting and habitat destruction reduced the herd to only fifty animals by 1950.

Although the number of deer has increased with the protection of the new refuge, road kills, injury, and dog attacks continue to take a toll. Construction of condominiums and private homes, swallowing up what used to be open land, has further restricted the habitat of the tiny deer.

broad, flat bills edged with tiny sawlike teeth and used by ducks to hold and strain food.

Ducks have feathers of many colors—from the brilliant green feathers of a mallard's head and the blue of the blue-winged teal to the rainbow of colors in the wood duck's plumage. A large gland just above the tail keeps their feathers well oiled with a substance that waterproofs duck feathers. Remove the oil from its plumage and a duck will not be able to stay afloat.

A duck's webbed feet make it a swift swimmer and diver but an awkward creature on land. It has strong wings; wild ducks can fly fast and far.

Ducks eat insects, snails, frogs, and fish. They also feed on grasses and other kinds of plant life.

The mother duck lays from six to sixteen eggs in a warm nest of leaves or dry grass. She plucks down feathers from her own breast to line the nest, which is close to water and hidden in high vegetation.

As soon as the newborn ducklings break through their shells, the mother duck covers them with down to hide them from predators such as turtles and raccoons. When her ducklings can walk she leads them to water, but it is six weeks before they can fly.

In early summer, after the breeding season, the male duck (drake) loses its brightly colored feathers and molts into drab plumage. It is then grounded and cannot fly until its new feathers grow in.

There are two major groupings of ducks:

Puddle ducks, or surface-feeding ducks, feed along the fringes of islands and shorelines and on dry land, eating seeds, grasses, leaves, and the stems of underwater plants, along with mollusks, insects, and fish. Species like the mallard, pintail, and black duck live in the shallows of lakes, rivers, and freshwater marshes, although they frequent salt water as well, especially during migrations. Puddle ducks are capable of springing straight out of the water into the air.

Diving ducks dive underwater as deep as thirty to forty feet to obtain aquatic plants, fish, insects, mollusks, and crustaceans. Their bodies are more compact than those of puddle ducks and they have less surface area to their wings. Instead of springing into the air as puddle ducks do, diving ducks, such as the canvasback, redhead, and goldeneye, must run across the water to build up speed before they can become airborne.

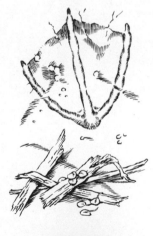

Swans and Geese

One of the most reliable signs of the changing seasons is the flight of the Canada goose, the most common variety of America's geese.

As a wildlife watcher you will have no trouble recognizing these honking birds as they fly in a V-shaped formation overhead—resolutely heading north in the

swan

Canada goose

spring and south in the fall. This hardy traveler undertakes migration journeys of up to four thousand miles.

In clear weather, wild geese often fly several thousand feet above the ground, perhaps even beyond earshot. On an overcast or foggy day they fly at much lower altitudes, giving the observer the full effect of their graceful flight and loud honking.

A flight of Canada geese seems to be led by an older, experienced bird. Younger geese are interspersed among older ones in the formation; the younger geese trail their elders, or follow their "slipstream," thus encountering less air resistance than the bird ahead and using less energy. The birds seem to fly in a V-formation to give each bird a clear view ahead.

A goose's legs are set farther forward on its body than those of a duck or a swan, permitting the goose to walk and graze better on dry land. A day's feeding by Canada geese usually fits a pattern. At dawn the birds leave the pond or impoundment where they have spent the night and fly to a feeding area, such as a cut-over cornfield, where they feed for two or three hours. They then return to the pond, rest, then fly out again to feed in the early evening. While feeding, one or more geese stands guard to give a warning if a predator appears. If in danger, the entire field of birds can take wing at once.

Canada geese are intelligent and wary. In regions where they are hunted, they seem to quickly learn the location and boundaries of refuges where they are protected. Surprisingly, there are probably more geese in the country today than when the first settlers arrived. Like certain other animal species such as crows, woodchucks, and white-tailed deer, Canada geese have benefited from the increased production of grain and cereal crops.

Other species of geese, such as the white-fronted goose, the blue goose, and the brant, also migrate with the seasons, following the Central and Pacific flyways.

Along the Atlantic coast the whistling swan joins the Canada goose to winter over in inlets from Maryland to North Carolina. The big white swan, half again as long as the Canada goose, has a black beak, legs, and feet, making it readily recognizable to observers. The high-pitched hooting of a flock of whistlers will reveal their presence long before you see them in the sky.

But you have to go to the West to see the largest of our native waterfowl, the dignified trumpeter swan. Once a threatened species, the trumpeter has staged a comeback. All white with a beak of black, the trumpeter grows to thirty pounds in weight with a wingspan of up to eight feet. Even from a distance, the bird's resonant bugling is distinct. Close up, the flight of these graceful birds is a glory of the sky.

Wildlife of the Prairies and Plains

Searching for wildlife in the prairies that stretch across the central part of the United States is a great deal different than it is in the leafy woodlands of the East or the watery empire of the South.

On these open plains many animals are readily visible. Since few trees or bushes interrupt the sweep of rolling hills and grasslands, animals find few places to hide. Thus, wild creatures must find other ways to protect themselves.

For the bison that is no problem. This shaggy beast is so large and powerful it has few rivals. The pronghorn, the fastest mammal in North America, relies on its speed, keen eyesight and sense of smell to avoid its enemies. Coyotes and mule deer take advantage of their protective coloration, yet they are still visible to the alert observer. Prairie dogs find safety in underground burrows.

These animals live in a region that owes much of its shape to the glaciers that scoured this midsection of the country during the Ice Age thousands of years ago, the same glaciers that gouged out the Great Lakes and flattened much of the continent.

In this great inland basin the quality of the soil and the amount of rain and snow determine the vegetation that will thrive and consequently the animals that can live there. To the north, in Michigan, Minnesota, and Wisconsin, forests cover much of the land, extending the eastern woodlands and providing a home for animals of the forests. In Nebraska, Iowa, Illinois, and Kansas, farmers have plowed up the prairie and cut down trees to plant corn, soybeans, and other crops. In North Dakota, South Dakota, and Colorado, wheat and corn production and cattle and hog raising predominate.

Only in parks and protected areas have the original grasslands of the Great Plains survived to provide habitat for the animals of the plains. Tall grasses grow where rain is plentiful in the eastern plains, midlength grasses grow in the region of moderate rainfall, and short grasses grow in the drier, western plains where the "rain shadow" of the Rocky Mountains keeps precipitation at a low level.

Bison

bison

We gained an insight into the variety and visibility of wildlife on the plains the morning we visited Hayden Valley in Yellowstone National Park. This world-renowned national park in the northwest corner of Wyoming lies at the prairie's western edge.

Getting off to a 6:45 A.M. start, we postponed breakfast in favor of trying to see wildlife in the prime early morning hours. In the chill a haze hung over the Yellowstone River and frost whitened the meadows.

Luck was with us. We quickly spotted a doe mule deer and its fawn standing at the edge of a wooded area and a frisky young moose in a meadow.

In the sky three ravens swooped over the valley and a flight of Canada geese made a pass overhead. One by one the geese peeled off from their V-formation to land on a lake where two dignified trumpeter swans preened to prepare for the day.

Then we saw the herd of some thirty bison grazing in the sagebrush and grass near the park tour road. A big bull caught our eye. It ambled across the road, causing us and other motorists to stop. Once on the other side it lowered its huge head and rubbed vigorously against a slender pine tree, bending the sapling almost to the ground.

Look for a tree like this: its bark partly rubbed off, pieces of the bison's curly brown hair caught in its trunk; it is a good indication of bison in the vicinity. Bison rub against trees and rocks a great deal in the spring to help them thin out their thick winter coat. They also wallow in dirt or mud, caking their flanks with dirt, possibly to protect themselves from biting insects.

As other animals in the herd crossed the road in front of us we got a strong impression of the massive size of this heaviest mammal of the North American continent. A large bull bison may stand six feet high at the shoulder and weigh a full ton. Its weight is concentrated in its forequarters, where its dark brown, shaggy hair is longest; its hindquarters are covered with shorter hair. Its heavily muscled neck supports a low-hung head with a thick forelock of hair. Behind its massive head a broad back rounds into a hump.

A female, or cow, bison averages a height of five feet at the shoulder and weighs only half as much as a bull. Both the bull and the cow have horns—with distinctions in shape. A bull's horns curve upward and are used as weapons of attack; a cow's horns curve but are more slender.

Incidentally, the proper name for this symbol of the American West is *bison*, although it is often popularly referred to as a "buffalo." True buffaloes, like the water buffalo, live in Asia and Africa and have different characteristics.

Suddenly, up on a hillside, a cloud of dust arose. Two aggressive bulls clashed, possibly contending over possession of a chosen cow. We could hear the sound of butting heads and horns. Each pawed the ground, kicking up swirls of dust, then lunged at the other. They backed up, then lunged again.

The heavy thuds made us cringe from half a mile away. But the contest ended after a minute or two of combat. The defeated bull turned its head aside, then turned away completely. Head lowered, it trotted off to try to best another bull and thus win a mate. A bull bison may lose some three hundred pounds during the rut, or mating season, from battling other bulls and from constantly accompanying, or "tending," a cow until she is ready to mate.

Thus is dominance demonstrated in a bison herd. Males that dominate other males gain the right to breed with the cows. Fighting is one means of establishing and maintaining dominance. But because fighting is dangerous and demands much time and energy, animals have developed alternatives to actual combat.

Watch a fascinating "bison ballet" at some prairie park and you will see how bulls establish a hierarchy without bloodshed. A bull snorts, stamps its foot, or bellows at a second bull. The second bull turns broadside to the first, drawing its body up to maximum size and bellowing; the first bull swings its head and neck widely to one side or lowers its head to graze—a sign of submission.

In spring a cow gives birth to a single calf that is bright tawny to buff in color and weighs between thirty and seventy pounds. The newborn can suckle immediately. Within a few minutes of birth it can stand, and in only three hours the newborn calf is able to run.

A cow is very protective of its young calf and keeps it close to her. A word of warning: Do not allow yourself to come between a bison cow and her calf; the cow may very likely demonstrate the tendency of a mother anywhere to protect its offspring. It could send you sprawling.

From late fall to spring a bison herd usually separates into two groups: cows and calves in one and older bulls in the other. The two groups, however, intermingle from time to time, drifting together, then splitting up again.

Bison normally feed five times a day: just before dawn, just before midday, in the middle of the afternoon, one to two hours before sunset, and again around midnight. Between feedings, herds rest, each animal regurgi-

tating and then rechewing its cud, the same way a domestic cow does. During the day the herd moves from
one feeding area to another or to a watering spot, usually led by an older cow. In the course of a day a herd will
travel within a radius of one to two miles, depending on
how close the water source is.

In their travels, bison frequently follow established
trails and do not hesitate to cross large, swift rivers.
Winter reports have described bison attempting to cross
thin ice and breaking through it. Hundreds of bison perish as the herd continues ever forward, the lead animals
pushed into the icy waters to drown.

Rangers agree that the best way to view bison is
from the safety of your car. You will often find, as we did,
a herd grazing on land near a roadway or a parking area.
You may be able to pull off the road or into the parking
area without disturbing the herd. You'll have a ringside
seat from which to watch.

Bison claim the right-of-way on the tour road at the National Bison Range in Montana. Drive wildlife
tour roads slowly and stop frequently at turnouts to scan the landscape with binoculars.

Get out your binoculars and plan to stay a while so that you can study the social interactions between animals and look for males trying to establish dominance. Be alert for the following interactions among bison in the herd: the lead cow maintaining its dominance, a bull tending a cow, a cow protecting its calf, a yearling (one-year-old) bull that is about ready to leave its mother and strike out on its own.

We observed a fascinating tableau one day at Wind Cave National Park. A bull was tending a cow, walking close behind or beside the female as they grazed together. The cow's yearling bull calf was with her as well. Every so often the calf ducked its head beneath its mother's stomach, seeking to nurse. In response, the cow gave its offspring a gentle kick with her hind leg, pushing it away. The cow seemed to be giving her young son a message: "You're getting too old to nurse and I'm busy with other things. Go graze for your lunch and leave me alone."

Listen, too, for the variety of sounds that bison make. You will hear assorted snorts and sneezes. A cow utters a series of sharp grunts like a pig when it wants to call her calf; the calf answers with a high-pitched grunt. But the most impressive bison sound is the booming bellow of the bull during the rut, a sound that has much in common with the roar of an African lion.

Rangers have a useful safety tip they pass along to those who observe the bison: pay close attention to the position of the animal's tail. A tail hanging loosely behind a bison indicates that the animal is relaxed. If the tail is partly raised, the bison is alert. If the tail is held out horizontally, the bison is excited. But if the tail points upward the bison is in a combative posture and may be ready to charge.

A raised tail is a warning to keep your distance. Any wild animal is potentially dangerous if it feels threatened. And a human approaching too closely can threaten an animal. Rangers advise caution even when a herd seems to be grazing quietly. Although a bull only rarely charges a visitor, it is best to keep about one hundred yards between you and this powerful animal.

Bison rely on their heavy coat of hair to tough it out over the cold prairie winters. Herds may seek the shelter of clumps of trees during a storm. To forage in winter, a bison sweeps aside the snow with its muzzle and digs down as deep as four feet to get at succulent grass.

There are a number of preserves in the West where you can view bison. Sizable herds can be found at Yellowstone National Park and Grand Teton National Park in Wyoming; the National Bison Range in Montana; Badlands National Park, Wind Cave National Park, and Custer State Park in South Dakota; Theodore Roosevelt National Park in North Dakota; Fort Niobrara National Wildlife Refuge in Nebraska; and Wichita Mountains National Wildlife Refuge in Oklahoma.

Pronghorn

pronghorn

The pronghorn, truly an American animal, is found nowhere else in the world. Often mistaken for an antelope, it is not a true antelope like the many African species. Instead, it is the sole survivor of a group of spiral- and fork-horned mammals that evolved millions of years ago in North America.

This remarkable resident of the West has another distinction as well: it is the swiftest mammal on the plains. A pronghorn can run fifty miles an hour for short distances when it's alarmed.

We had our best view of the speedy pronghorn on the open grasslands of the National Bison Range in Montana. The Bison Range, although established for one of the first federally protected herds of bison, also preserves large numbers of pronghorn, bighorn sheep, elk, mule deer, and white-tailed deer.

As we leisurely drove the tour road one afternoon, about twenty pronghorns came up a slope to our left and slowly crossed the road in front of us one and two at a time, paying no attention to our motor home. We stopped to let them trot across the roadway and bound up a steep bank on the other side. The windshield provided an unplanned yet perfect blind from which to get a close-up view of these graceful speedsters.

The pronghorn is about the size of the mule deer and white-tailed deer but its physical characteristics are quite different. The pronghorn's coat is cinnamon brown, sometimes seeming almost orange, quite unlike the gray brown of both the muley and the white-tail. The pronghorn's flanks, underparts, and rump are white; white on the mule deer and white-tail is limited to the patch on their rump.

White flanks and rump and white stripes on the pronghorn's neck are telltale signs when you see a herd of pronghorns across the prairie. If spooked, the animal raises the hairs on its rump patch to form two white rosettes. Flashing in the sunlight as the animal flees, the rosettes catch the eye of other pronghorns as far away as a mile or two, warning them of potential danger.

The coarse outer guard hairs of its coat provide it with insulation against cold winds that whistle across the prairie in winter. Held flat against the body, these hairs conserve body heat. When weather warms, the pronghorn lifts the hairs of its coat, allowing air to circulate to cool its body.

The pronghorn has a broader face than mule deer or white-tailed deer. Its eyes protrude from its skull and give it excellent peripheral vision toward the rear as well as ahead. These remarkable eyes are the equivalent of eight-power binoculars—they allow the pronghorn to spot a moving object on the prairie up to four miles away.

As we could see from our front row seats, the name pronghorn is a perfect description for this animal. A pair of horns rise from the top of its head, curving inward at the tips. It is the only animal in the world to regularly shed the sheaths on its horns and renew them. The horn sheaths are shed in the late fall after the rut; they grow back over the winter and spring. Female pronghorns (does) have either no horns at all or smaller horns than the bucks.

The slender pronghorn manages to subsist on the scant vegetation offered by the short-grass prairie and sagebrush flats of the western states, particularly Wyoming and Montana where the largest populations live.

This creature prefers leafy plants like clover, lupine, and cut-leaf daisy and is particularly fond of flowers and the sweet prickly pear cactus. It will eat almost any vegetation including Russian thistle, loco weed, and poison vetch, all of which are not touched by other animals. Its comparatively large liver breaks down the toxins in these plants and makes them digestible.

When winter comes, pronghorns migrate as much as one hundred miles to find a place where winds have blown the snow from the landscape. There it browses on sagebrush, rabbitbush, cedar, and other shrubs. If forced to forage in snow, it brushes the snow aside with its forefeet to find good greens.

Distinctive antlers and white markings on the neck, underbelly, and rump make it easy to distinguish the pronghorn from the white-tailed deer and mule deer, which are about the same size.

An adult male breaks away from the main herd in spring to stake out an individual territory, where it tries to attract a group of does for its harem. A courting buck performs an elaborate assortment of mating rituals: prancing, swinging its head, erecting the hairs of its mane and rump patch, smacking its lips, and whining. As a final ploy, it offers the doe a sniff of a gland lying beneath a patch of black hair below each ear.

Dominant bucks select the best forage sites and protect their prime territory from other males. To challenge another male, a buck resorts to another collection of tactics: staring, wheezing, grinding its teeth, or actually challenging the other to a fight in which they spar with pronged horns.

The young, usually twins, appear in May or June. Weighing from four to six pounds apiece, each lies in a separate hiding place where the doe gave birth. Their soft color blends in with the dusty background. Should a coyote wander too close, the mother pronghorn tries to lure the predator away. Within a week the newborns are able to run faster than a man and begin to accompany their mother in her wanderings. The does band together with other females and kids to assure mutual safety and companionship.

Millions of pronghorns roamed the plains when covered wagons brought settlers west, but by 1910 the species had seriously dwindled. A high reproductive rate and protection in wildlife preserves has helped the pronghorn recover from a population low of about fifteen thousand to an estimated five hundred thousand today.

Mule Deer

Since several million mule deer populate the western prairie states, your chances of bringing a mule deer into focus in your binoculars are excellent. They are the most widely distributed and abundant of all species of large mammals native to western North America.

Helpful rangers will be glad to tell you where to look. Although the gray brown mule deer blends in with its surroundings, you can often separate the animal from the background by looking for movement—up a draw or along a forest edge where a muley might be feeding. Best times to look are early morning or at dusk, when deer come out of the trees to browse near the tree line, in a forest's grassy clearing, or in a meadow.

Look for small herds of several does and their fawns, which often browse together. Bucks forage by themselves and lead a solitary life, except before and during the rut when they join up with the doe-fawn herds.

In the West the ranges of mule deer and white-tailed deer overlap. It's a challenge to tell the two apart but you

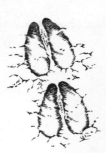

mule deer

A car window serves as a window on wildlife. This mule deer wandered up to the motor home as the author and his wife sat having dinner at a picnic area at Wind Cave National Park in South Dakota. A vehicle is often a good blind.

should soon be able to do so by comparing their habitat, size, ears, tails, and antlers.

Look for the mule deer along a forest edge or on open grasslands, but look for the white-tail within the forest itself (although some white-tailed deer become accustomed to people and are found around lodges and campgrounds).

The mule deer is more solidly built and is about 3 to 3½ feet high at the shoulder and up to 6½ feet long; the white-tail is more slender and is about 2¾ feet to 3½ feet high at the shoulder and 6 feet long.

A mule deer's ears, from which it derives its name, are two-thirds the length of its head and protrude prominently; a white-tail's are smaller and more pointed.

The muley's tail is white with a black tip; the white-tail's is black down its center, edged with white, and completely white underneath, forming the "flag" that rises to warn other deer at a time of alarm.

Finally, the antlers of a mule deer buck fork into two equal branches as they rise upward from its head. The antlers of a white-tailed deer rise upward on one main beam, then separate into branches toward the top.

A mule deer's ears are remarkable. Not only can both ears swivel in about a 270-degree arc, but the deer can listen to one sound with one ear, simultaneously rotating the other ear to catch a sound coming from another direction. It can even pick up sounds coming from directly behind.

One ranger told us he was hiking along a ridgeline when he spotted several mule deer browsing near the trail. As he continued, he recalled, he could see the animals' ears following his movements from one side to the other—like a battery of radar antennas tracking a target.

It is the unique characteristic of stotting, however, that sets the mule deer apart from other deer. When it senses danger, the mule deer performs a stiff-legged bound, bringing all four feet off the ground at the same time. It can stot either from a standstill or while running.

To evade a predator, it can travel up to twenty-six feet in a single leap and clear an obstacle six feet high. It can turn its body completely around in midair to reverse direction. Using these great leaps, it bounds upslope rather than down, leaping over bushes and rocks, making it very difficult for a pursuer to follow.

A mule deer's diet varies with the food that is available. Studies show that a deer can consume any of some eight hundred different kinds of plants, including grasses, herbs, berries, shrubs, and both deciduous and coniferous tree twigs and leaves.

During spring and summer the deer finds plenty to eat, feasting on new growth and ripening leaves and berries, putting on the fat that will help carry it over winter. Then, when plants are dormant, the deer is reduced to eating evergreens, bushes, and deciduous trees such as sagebrush, juniper, aspen, willow, dogwood, huckleberry, Douglas fir, and western cedar. Bacteria in the deer's stomach break down this seemingly indigestible material into the proteins, fats, and carbohydrates that give it nourishment.

Doe mule deer usually bear twin fawns in June or July, carefully depositing each spotted fawn in separate well-hidden locations. The mother forages for food, returning to feed her fawns in their respective hiding places about every four hours. The little ones are able to nibble succulent shoots in a few days and can run after their mother in three weeks. If you have sharp eyes, you may be able to spot the matted-down place where a deer has bedded down.

By following suggestions from rangers and by scanning the roadside as we drove, we succeeded in viewing our share of mule deer during a seven-week trip through ten western states. For example:

- At dinner one evening at Wind Cave two mule deer does browsed through our picnic area to within a few feet of our motor home; we watched them through our widescreen windshield.

- While taking an early morning drive at the suggestion of a ranger at Glacier National Park, we saw a black bear and its cub crossing the road. Then in succession we watched four individual mule deer does and one fawn browsing near the roadside.

- While hiking a trail at Rocky Mountain National Park we suddenly came upon a doe and her fawn ahead of us on the trail. As soon as they heard us, the pair bounded off the path and into the forest.

- When we stopped one day at Yellowstone to make a "binocular sweep," as we did frequently, Marge spotted a rack of antlers about half a mile away. It was a buck mule deer resting under a tree. The sighting proved the value in looking for parts of animals, as one ranger advised.

- We observed an unusual characteristic of mule deer at Badlands National Park. Looking up a gully we saw a mule deer stot, or bounce straight up in the air as if propelled by a coiled spring under each hoof, bounding up an embankment to escape our intrusion.

Coyote

One day we stopped to glance out over an expanse of sagebrush in Yellowstone National Park. At first we saw nothing. But when Marge lifted her binoculars she caught sight of a coyote a hundred yards away. We had long been looking for this animal, whose grizzled gray coat blends so well with its surroundings.

As we watched, the coyote began to stalk its prey. Head down, nose sniffing the ground, tail pressed against its rump, body taut, it cocked its head first to one side, then to the other.

Inching ahead step by careful step, it listened and tried to sense underground vibrations with its footpads. All at once it leaped upward, all four feet in the air, and pounced on its quarry—a luckless vole. Shaking the rodent vigorously, it lifted its head and gulped down the vole in two swallows.

We had just witnessed the skill of one of nature's most cunning and resourceful hunters, the so-called brush wolf of the prairie.

Rangers say it will eat almost anything, but its chief food is rodents. Coyote predation helps keep rodent populations in balance. Coyotes also consume rabbits, ground-nesting birds, dead animals, reptiles, amphibians, fish, insects, grass, and fruits. Biologists say about ninety percent of a coyote's consumption consists of mammals.

Its undiscriminating appetite has given the coyote a bad name with ranchers and farmers who accuse it of attacking sheep, calves, and chickens. Although such reports have undoubtedly been exaggerated, livestock

coyote

owners and hunters for many years have shot, trapped, and poisoned coyotes to get rid of these so-called varmints. Even federal agents participate in this war against the coyote. Between 1937 and 1969 federal predator control agents killed no less than 2,823,000 coyotes in response to pleas for action by sheep raisers; such anti-coyote actions still continue today.

In spite of the campaign against the coyote, this adaptable animal has actually expanded its range. Within the past thirty years coyotes have infiltrated the Midwest and the Northeast and have recently been reported in the Middle Atlantic and Southeastern states.

The coyote is about as big as a medium-size domestic dog, but only about half the size of a gray wolf. Its shaggy, gray brown coat shades into a whitish underbelly. Coarse guard hairs cover a soft underfur that keeps the animal warm. Its pointed ears face forward. It often carries its bushy tail down close to its body, as distinct from most dogs, whose tails are typically horizontal or almost vertical.

In its food-gathering activities, the coyote patrols throughout its home range, using its keen sense of sight, smell, and hearing to locate prey. Coyotes sometimes pair up or form packs to hunt large animals or defend their territory.

Coyotes are smart. The Crow Indians called them "tricksters." One ranger provided an example of the coyote's resourcefulness. He watched one day as a badger started digging at the entrance to a pocket gopher's burrow. A coyote waited nearby, watching. While the badger dug furiously at the gopher's "front door," the coyote pounced on the rodent as it tried to escape from a "back door," the gopher's emergency burrow exit.

The coyote's howl is legendary—a true symbol of the West. Its song has a higher pitch than that of the wolf.

One evening as dusk settled over a wilderness campground at Badlands, Marge and I heard the howl of several coyotes from behind a tree line. A coyote's howl can take several forms, but this night it was a lengthy yowl-l-l-l followed by several yip-yip-yips. One author describes the call of the coyote as "a prolonged howl which the animal lets out and then runs after and bites into small pieces."

Biologists believe that howling serves several purposes for a coyote. It puts a coyote in contact with other coyotes, inspiring group members for a prospective hunt. It rallies straggling members of a pack. And it could be a warning to nonmembers of a pack to stay out of its territory.

At several national parks, rangers imitate the coyote's call, trying to goad an animal into responding. It's a thrill to take part in such a conversation between a ranger and a wild animal. Coyotes sometimes even approach to investigate a simulated mouse squeak or the scream of a rabbit in distress when the ranger aims his tape recorder at a nearby forest.

Unlike many animals, coyotes seem to mate for life. They breed in February, the female giving birth to a litter of five to ten pups in her den in April. The den is often located in the roots of an old tree, in a bank, or on a hillside. Coyotes often keep several dens, using the same ones from year to year.

When the pups are old enough to take solid food, they are fed by both parents. They begin to play at the entrance to their den at about three to four weeks of age and by ten weeks leave the den completely. If the den is threatened by people, the parents transfer the family to new quarters sometimes as far as five miles away.

By late summer the young coyotes accompany their parents on their nightly rounds. Both parents teach the young how to hunt. By fall the youngsters, nearly as large as their parents, are ready to begin life on their own.

Badger

You can consider yourself fortunate if you should happen to see a badger, because these hard-working, deep-digging animals do most of their hunting in the dark of night and out of sight beneath the ground.

The badger is a born digger—and a good one. With its wide, squat body, short neck, and wedge-shaped head, it presents a low profile. Silver gray to brown in color, it has a white stripe from shoulder to pointed snout and white markings on its face. Its short, powerful legs are tipped with two-inch curved and pointed claws used to tunnel into the earth.

When the badger catches the scent of a ground squirrel, chipmunk, or prairie dog, it rips into its victim's burrow entrance with powerful strokes of its clawed forelimbs. The left front and right hind leg work together, alternating with the other two limbs, as the badger shoves the dirt behind it out of the hole. As it digs, the flattened body of the badger seems to sink out of sight.

Once below ground, the burrowing badger is guided to the correct tunnel by its sense of smell. It snorts loudly from time to time to clear its nostrils and catch a fresh scent of its prey. A thin movable membrane protects its eyes from gritty dust, and fringes of hair keep soil particles from entering its ear cavities. It continues digging in a burrow for many minutes—until it reaches its prey or until its victim escapes via an alternate tunnel entrance.

When we visited the historic Cunningham Cabin in Grand Teton National Park, the home of an early settler in the upper Snake River Valley, we came across perhaps two dozen badger holes shaped like half-moons. A champion digger had evidently gone after a whole bunch of Uinta ground squirrels in the soft, sandy soil.

badger

So adept a digger is the badger that it often concludes a day's work by digging itself a new den right at the work site and holing up there until it resumes digging the following morning. Badger tunnels reach thirty feet in length and descend to five feet or more in depth.

In the unlikely event that you should come face to face with a badger, you would quickly discover another of its characteristics—it is a tenacious fighter and a superb escape artist. Despite its reputation for toughness, however, badgers seldom pick a fight, preferring, like most mammals, to retreat.

Here is how Bill Mullendore, a wildlife specialist with the Michigan Department of Natural Resources, describes an encounter with a badger: "I suspect that I stepped directly upon its den and the animal came out to see what was intruding upon its territory.

"A mature badger is afraid of nothing, including people, and can always hold its own against any predator—a dog, coyote, fox, hawk, or owl. Few small animals are so immune to attack.

"The creature avoided my foot by scuttling to one side, then turned to confront me. Hissing and growling through bared teeth, the badger put on a show of bravery remarkable for an animal the size of a small dog threatened by a being ten times its size.

"We stared at each other for maybe half a minute, then my feisty antagonist broke the spell. A flurry of feet and a flying of dirt and suddenly the strange-looking beast wasn't there any more. It had dug itself out of sight!"

The badger has another defense against attacking animals—it can twist around in its own skin to evade a bite, then get in a bite of its own. Its rubbery skin hangs so loosely that it appears to belong to a larger animal, making it difficult for an attacker to get a killing grip. For its part, a badger's bite is strong enough to bite through a man's hand.

A resident of the grasslands and sagebrush country, the badger lives a solitary life except during August and September's mating season, when males search for females in heat. An average of three to seven young are born in March or April in a den deep underground.

The eyes of the newborn open after four weeks. Young badgers soon begin to gnaw on prey brought into the den by their mother. After six weeks they appear above ground for the first time. Soon they can fend for themselves, leaving home at the early age of ten to twelve weeks.

Prairie Dog

The prairie dog is the answer to a wildlife-watcher's dream. Unlike many of the animals you encounter in the wild, the prairie dog is more or less predictable.

prairie dog

You can find out ahead of time where they live, you can readily observe them, you will find them active during the day—and you will discover that they are fascinating animals to watch.

Prairie dogs live in dry, upland prairies, preferring flat land that offers a good view of their surroundings. There are notable prairie dog "towns" at the Charles M. Russell National Wildlife Refuge in Montana, Badlands National Park and Wind Cave National Park in South Dakota, and the Wichita Mountains National Wildlife Refuge in Oklahoma.

The prairie dog, of course, is not a dog; it is a rodent, one of the gnawing animals. It got its misleading name when early French explorers named the light tan rodent *petit chien* (little dog).

Before the plow cut into the Great Plains in the late nineteenth century, millions of prairie dogs inhabited the region between the Alleghenies and the Rockies. In 1905 there were an estimated eight hundred million prairie dogs in Texas alone.

Ranchers and farmers poisoned and killed thousands of the animals for two reasons: they claimed the rodents ate grass needed to fatten steers, and their horses and cows injured limbs by stumbling over burrow openings. In fact, prairie dogs eat many weeds that cattle will not touch, and their burrow mounds aerate the soil.

The ranchers' attitude persists, however, and prairie dogs have many opponents. For example, we drove by a campground in South Dakota that offered "free prairie dog shooting" to any overnight guest.

Now prairie dogs thrive mainly on protected lands, including the four national parks and wildlife refuges noted above. The rodent's activity, you soon realize, goes on both above and below the ground—whether you can see it or not. Valerie Naylor, a park ranger, reminded us of that fact the day we went looking for prairie dogs at Badlands.

"'Does anything live out here?' people ask when they first arrive," she said. "They see acres and acres of prairie and very little apparent animal life. But after they've gone to a prairie dog town and watched for awhile they get a better understanding of how active this animal community is."

At first sight the Roberts Prairie Dog Town does look like just another section of flat prairie. Peering more closely, we noted a scattering of miniature craters, each hole surrounded by a circular mound of earth. We also noticed that the grass was cropped short where the rodents had eaten it or carried it away to their underground nests. Then we saw a sentinel prairie dog twenty to thirty yards in front of us, sitting on its haunches on one of the mounds. It cocked its head to one side to listen, got down on all fours, then popped up again, emitting a chirping alarm to warn its fellow prairie dogs of a trespasser.

Prairie dogs have plenty to warn each other about. Numerous predators are ready to attack them from either the sky or the ground. They fear the eagle, hawk, owl, falcon, coyote, swift fox, badger, bobcat, snake and—until most of them were killed by man—the black-footed ferret.

The underground part of the prairie dog's burrow is an elaborate network of tunnels at the base of a "plunge shaft" that drops six to twelve feet from the mounded entrance, then levels out. A side chamber near the entrance gives the animal a listening post where it can hide while waiting for a coyote to trot away, a hawk to fly on, or a human visitor to leave. Other chambers off the main tunnel hold a nest for young and a toilet chamber.

Prairie dog groups, known as "coteries," typically consist of one adult male, three or four adult females, and offspring less than one year of age. Each coterie occupies a particular "neighborhood" within a prairie dog town. Residents of each coterie protect their territory from intruders, including prairie dogs from other coteries.

These busy rodents are social creatures that exhibit a high degree of cooperation. All the members of a coterie seem to occupy a nearly equal social position and do not compete with each other for food and shelter.

Members of a coterie often recognize each other with a "kiss" and are quick to eject trespassers who are not members of the same select circle. They also groom each other, cooperate to dig out a burrow, aid each other in defense of their territory, eat together, frolic with one another, and stand side by side at their burrow entrances.

The prairie dog's dreaded foes are the badger, who can dig it out, and the ferret, who can pursue it underground. To foil them the rodent digs an escape tunnel that extends almost to the ground surface. In an emergency it escapes by clawing through the last few inches of soil to the surface. Should rain flood the burrow, the prairie dog heads for its escape tunnel, which can also serve as an air lock.

As we walked through the town we could hear the prairie dog warning system at work as one sentinel after another chirped its alarm, always well ahead of us. Biologists have identified ten distinct prairie dog calls with various purposes. By making a clicking noise with its teeth, a prairie dog signals belligerence or frustration; a rasping noise indicates an imminent attack; a high-pitched scream denotes pain; and a jump in the air together with a *yip* indicates an "all clear" after a period of danger.

On a warm, sunny day prairie dogs cautiously emerge from their burrows to nibble on grass, weeds, roots, and seeds, or to collect grass to take underground for their nests. They do not come out at night—that is

Two black-tailed prairie dogs assume a sitting position as they nibble tender shoots. Prairie dogs build their burrows on flat land where they have an unobstructed view of an approaching predator.

when their enemies, such as the badger and the owl, might be around.

Prairie dog breeding season is from mid-March to mid-April; the young are born four to five weeks later in litters of two to eight. Young prairie dogs are nursed by mothers for about six weeks. When their eyes open at roughly five weeks, the youngsters begin to explore their burrow.

At six weeks they venture outside for the first time to forage, tumble, and play in the sunshine. Their mother schools them and pushes them into the burrow if an alarm sounds.

Prairie dogs are tolerated outside their own coterie while they are too young to know better; later they will be chased off. Soon they set up housekeeping in vacant holes, staking claims with much yipping. Standing up to declare their territorial rights, their bodies jerk with the vehemence of their barks; they sometimes even fall over backwards.

At this time, yearlings (youngsters from the previous year) and some adults may relocate, taking over unused burrows or digging new burrows at the edge of the town. A few daring individuals might even travel a mile or more in search of a new area, but the risk is high; once away from the communal warning system most are easy prey for predators. But relocation of the older prairie dogs leaves the well-used burrows to the young pups, who feel both socially and structurally secure in them.

Our quiet observation of the Roberts Prairie Dog Town was interrupted by an unexpected visitor. A bull bison came wandering through, grazing as it shuffled along. We retreated to our motor home, allowing the bison its full territorial rights.

Bison such as this one, we discovered, often come to the prairie dog towns to roll in dirt left exposed by the entrance mounds and short grass. The prairie dogs simply endure this indignity—since there is nothing they can do about it—and rebuild their burrow entrances after the bison departs.

Prairie Chicken

Observing prairie dogs at their towns on the prairie is easy, but trying to glimpse the elusive prairie chicken is more of a challenge.

Prairie chickens, once abundant over much of the Great Plains, have diminished in number in the face of several factors. Much of their grassland habitat has been converted from open prairie to farmland. Widespread shooting by market hunters and sportsmen has killed off many of the birds. And finally, ring-necked pheasants, introduced into the United States as an exotic species for hunting, have crowded out many of the prairie chickens. But scattered across the Plains states are a number of preserves where you can still locate these upland birds and witness one of the most elaborate courtship rituals in the animal kingdom—the springtime display of the male prairie chicken.

Wildlife preserves where you can view the prairie chicken include the Flint Hills National Wildlife Refuge in Kansas; the Muleshoe National Wildlife Refuge, Aransas National Wildlife Refuge, and the Attwater Prairie Chicken National Wildlife Refuge in Texas; the Fort Pierce National Grasslands in North Dakota; two grassland sanctuaries in Illinois operated jointly by the Nature Conservancy and the state; as well as state refuges in Nebraska, Wisconsin, Missouri, and Minnesota.

prairie chicken

The prairie chicken resembles a husky, short-tailed pheasant. It is yellowish brown, with black spots on its upper parts and an underside of dusky brown with a pattern of white bars. Its tail is short and rounded.

During the spring mating season this typically conservative inhabitant of the prairie becomes its champion exhibitionist.

It all begins as day breaks over a stretch of prairie the size of a city block. The site is most likely an open ridge or open level terrain with good cover for nesting available nearby. This is the "booming ground" where the male prairie chicken struts his stuff; most likely, he has performed at the same location in earlier years.

Each male takes over a small area of the booming ground, an area he has previously fought for and won.

He starts to dance—dashing forward, head down, tail high, his wingtips dragging on the grass. He stamps a tattoo with his feet, pivoting, at the same time raising two tufts on his neck that look like horns. Now two vivid orange air sacs balloon outward from the sides of his neck—they are called *tympani*, or drums.

Soon you hear a sound you will never forget, a sound you hear only on the prairie. A hollow *whoo-hoo-hoo* booms from the bird's inflated throat sacs, a sound that observers say they can hear from a mile away on a clear, calm morning.

The foot-stomping dance continues. The bird flutters its feathers, whoops, cackles, clicks its tail feathers, even leaps a foot or so off the ground and lands facing in the opposite direction. He bluffs a charge at a nearby male, then retreats.

All this display seems to be an effort to impress the females, who watch from the sidelines. They now come out of the nearby cover and step through the bedlam of the booming ground. All the males rush to show off, scrambling for position, hooting, stomping, fighting, and jumping up and down. Unimpressed, the hens straggle through the area and head back to high cover. Soon after sunrise, all the birds leave.

This courtship ritual continues for days until the cocks eventually mate with the hens. Then each hen heads for tall grass cover where she hollows out a well-hidden nest, lays a dozen brown-flecked olive eggs, and raises her brood on a diet of bugs, berries, seeds, leaves, and grain.

During fall and winter prairie chickens flock in groups of as many as fifty, roosting in grassy cover or in the stubble of a field of grain. In winter a prairie chicken manages to stay warm even in snow. It digs five to ten inches beneath the snow's surface, then tunnels horizontally for a foot or so, hollowing out a roosting place in the snowbank. This talent, plus its ability to digest woody buds, gives the prairie chicken an advantage in wintering ability over quail and pheasants.

The prairie chicken is one of eighteen species of the grouse family. Grouse are distinguished by air sacs on their necks and by the feathers that cover their lower legs and nostrils. Other members of this ground-nesting bird family that you might see include the ruffed grouse and the ptarmigan.

Quail and Pheasant

This family of chickenlike birds, like their cousins the grouse, make their nests on the ground and take to the air only occasionally. Quail generally are smaller than grouse and do not sport feathers on their legs.

In some parts of the country, particularly the South, this plump game bird is known as a partridge. Two of the

quail

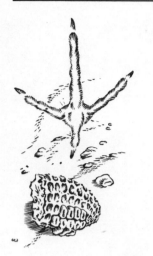

pheasant

most common species of quail in the United States are the bobwhite and the ring-necked pheasant.

In fall and winter, bobwhites gather in coveys or groups. The popular name for this bird derives from its call, which sounds like *ah-bob-white*. The covey travels on foot through fields and woods, the birds walking quietly while hidden by the cover. If they need to cross an opening in woods or fields, they run with necks extended and crests raised.

If you disturb a quail, it either runs out of the brush where it is hiding or erupts in a flutter of wings. Once an intruder has departed, bobwhites begin clucking in low voices to each other, signaling the covey to reassemble.

As evening nears the covey enters into thick underbrush. There the birds roost in a compact circle, heads pointing outward, tails toward the center, using each other's bodies to keep warm. This configuration allows the birds to take off immediately in an emergency without colliding with each other.

Bobwhite populations have decreased in recent years. As farming has become more mechanized, fields have grown larger. They have fewer edges of high grass and weeds, which provide quail and other wildlife with good feeding areas and protective cover.

The ring-necked pheasant has a long pointed tail and more colorful plumage than the bobwhite. The male has the trademark greenish black iridescent head and a mixture of brown, gold, and black feathers. A white ring runs around its neck below its head.

The hen has a more muted plumage of brown, black, and gray feathers that provide it with the camouflage to stay hidden in grass or underbrush.

The ring-necked pheasant, originally imported into the United States from China, flourishes throughout much of the country. The bird is extremely wary in autumn, staying in dense cover. During spring and summer it is more likely to be seen strutting across freshly mown fields and along roadsides. When pursued, a ring-neck runs rather than flies, dodging nimbly into cover such as brambles, honeysuckle, or a multiflora rose bush.

When cornered or surprised, it takes to the air. A strong flier for a short distance, it can attain a maximum speed of forty-five miles per hour.

Quail, like grouse, go through an involved mating routine, which is not as elaborate as the prairie chicken. The male ring-necked pheasant struts before the hens, turning this way and that to display its brilliant plumage to best advantage, walking with an exaggerated bobbing motion. Sometimes he runs in a circle around a hen, leaning in her direction, dragging the tip of one wing on the ground.

By such displays the cock lures the hen to its crowing area, a territory he has fought for and uses to collect his harem. A cock's harem may include two to five hens or more.

Although the ring-necked pheasant is commonly found in most states of the Midwest and some of the East, its populations have declined from their peaks in the 1920s and 1930s. Some states are taking action to arrest any further decline in numbers of this popular game bird. In Illinois, for example, the number of pheasants in the east-central part of the state decreased dramatically as farmers shifted from growing grain crops to raising large-scale crops of corn and soybeans. To bring back the pheasants, the state department of conservation will seed roadsides along a farmer's land with grasses that provide enough cover for pheasants to lay their eggs and protect them.

The state will seed the ribbon of land free of charge if the landowner agrees not to mow the grass until August, when the eggs will have hatched. As a result of this "Roadsides for Wildlife" program—financed by state hunting fees and federal excise taxes on sporting guns and ammunition—the pheasant population in a sixteen-county area of Illinois has tripled.

Conservation programs such as this one in Illinois have two benefits—increasing wildlife populations and making it easier for the traveling public to see wildlife close at hand in its natural habitat.

CHAPTER 8

Wildlife of
the Western Mountains

Our horses stood patiently as each of us swung up into the saddle, preparing to take a trail ride into the high country of the Rocky Mountains. Tony, our trail guide, checked the height of our stirrups and pulled at the cinches, then led our group out of the corral and onto the trail.

We were getting an introduction to the wildlife of the Rockies by taking a winding six-mile horseback trip to a rough-hewn chalet on a sixty-six hundred foot plateau in Glacier National Park's interior. At this elevation we hoped to gain a good vantage point for seeing agile mountain goats. We had so far seen them only with our binoculars from the valleys below as small white dots on the mountainsides.

As we progressed along the stony trail with four other riders, we became better acquainted with these mountains. The national park lies near the midpoint of the extensive Rocky Mountain chain that stretches through western Canada and the western United States, eventually dwindling into the deserts of the Southwest. Some of its jagged peaks stand eleven thousand feet above surrounding prairies and plains. Unlike the lower Appalachian Mountains of the East, a number of Rocky Mountain peaks remain covered with snow and ice all year.

Our climb took us through a thirty-five hundred-foot increase in altitude. Changes in vegetation signaled that we were passing through several life zones, biological environments where average temperature and precipitation determine what plants will grow.

Our ride began in the low light of a dense forest of hemlock and cedar, where the noise of the horses' hooves was muffled by a thick layer of pine needles covering the ground. We then moved through a zone of tall but scattered conifers, where the sunlight broke through from place to place, encouraging the growth of low shrubs and bushes. Next was a subalpine zone, where rocky slopes were dotted with occasional stands of fir trees and low bushes. Finally we reached the alpine tundra, where trees were absent entirely and the rocky mountainside was covered only with grass, moss, and small plants.

The vegetation in each life zone determines which animals can live there. Animals like elk and deer graze on the lower slopes in spring and summer, then migrate down to the valleys for the winter where they can find good browse from shrubs and escape the deep snow of the high country.

The mountain goats who live in the alpine zone derive their nourishment from sparse mountain vegetation. Their heavy coats of fur and hair protect them from winter wind and snow.

After three hours on horseback, which found us negotiating several tight switchbacks and watering our steeds when we crossed two mountain streams, we dismounted at Sperry Chalet to spend the night. But before we could relax, we had to complete our mission: observe the hardy mountain goats in their natural habitat.

Mountain Goat

Pulling on hiking boots and grabbing our trail packs, we headed up the trail to Sperry Glacier, hoping to see mountain goats on their own turf.

The trail led along mountain flanks, across meadows of subalpine fir, over tumbling streams, even up a stairway cut into a rock wall. Occasionally we stopped to catch our breath. At one stop hikers descending from the glacier assured us that several mountain goats were grazing at the upper levels.

At eight thousand feet the slope leveled out to a sort of plateau. Cradled in the rocky terrain were two alpine lakes, their blue gray water fed by the snowbank on the slope above them.

We took a breath to enjoy the scene. Just then two mountain goats, a nanny and her kid, appeared atop a rock shelf. They stepped down deliberately to an expanse of grass that stretched along the level where we sat. Without a glance, the goats grazed slowly toward us.

We sat still. We knew that if we remained on or below their level, the goats might accept our presence. If we moved to a higher level we would undoubtedly spook them—a goat's safest escape route from a predator is to head for higher ground where the predator will find it difficult to follow. The mother and kid grazed past, coming within twenty feet of us, then moving down to another grassy shelf, eventually disappearing around a rock outcropping.

mountain goat

Watching them, we realized that the terraces on which mountain goats graze are wider than we had imagined when viewing them through our binoculars from far below in the valley.

The encounter gave us a good look at this nimble mountaineer, which averages three feet in height and weighs from one hundred to three hundred pounds. Its long white coat, long beard, and slender backward-curving horns give it a dignified appearance. Under its coarse outer coat is a dense woolly underfur three to four inches deep; the two coats keep the animal warm even in subzero temperatures on windy mountains. In summer, mountain goats shed their outer coat and some of the underfur.

Strangely enough, biologists say that the mountain goat is not a true goat but is instead a relative of the antelope family that has adapted to living at high elevations. You can determine a goat's age from its horns, which continue to grow throughout its life. The horn grows throughout the year, except in winter, when growth stops because food intake is reduced; this non-growth period appears as a ring around the horn. Like the concentric layers of wood in a tree trunk, each ring represents a year's growth; counting the rings determines the animal's age.

The mountain goat scales dizzying heights—and seems to do so just for the fun of it. It is aided by a distinctive foot structure that provides a sure footing. The bottom pads of its two-toed hooves are composed of spongy material in a concave shape that provides suction against the climbing surface. For additional traction, the goat also can spread its toes apart to provide a greater surface for gripping.

A goat does not panic when its high ledge trails off into space, leaving it no room to turn. It either rears up and adroitly executes an about-face, or pulls itself up to another ledge. At treacherous crossings, a group of goats strings out in single file, sandwiching the kids between the adults.

Goats are both grazers and browsers. They feed on grasses, sedges, rushes, ferns, mosses, and lichens—the hardy alpine vegetation that withstands winter freezing, summer drought, intense sunlight, and months of being covered with snow. They nibble on shrubs such as huckleberry, currant, and bearberry.

When winter comes in, they turn to buds and twigs of shrubs and trees such as subalpine fir. They crave minerals and will travel a long way to reach a salt lick that provides them with the sodium their bodies need.

The males, or billy goats, give up their solitary existence during the rutting season in November and December to join small herds of females and kids. Males then become possessive and will fight other intruding males, swiping at their opponents with their horns.

A footsore hiker who arrives at the alpine mountaintops of Glacier National Park is rewarded with the thrilling sight of a nanny mountain goat and her kid grazing near a glacial lake.

Soon after mating, the female drives the male away, which is nature's way of dispersing the goat population. The billies must find food farther afield, leaving the home range to the nannies and their new offspring.

In spring, six months after mating, the nanny gives birth to a single kid, or occasionally twins. Barely ten minutes after birth the infant goat can stand; within thirty minutes it can jump.

Frigid winter weather takes a severe toll on newborn mountain goats. As many as eight of ten kids perish over winter, some because of exposure to the cold and wind, others because of golden eagles that sweep along the mountainsides and are strong enough to snatch a baby kid.

Following our mountaintop encounter with the nanny and kid, Marge and I had one other experience with these sure-footed animals. Back at Sperry Chalet we were returning to our cabin on a dark night, flashlight in hand, when our light beam caught a white apparition in the blackness. Startled, we took a second to realize that a group of goats had wandered into the camp area, probably looking for something tastier to eat than the sparse grass and plants of the mountain.

We looked at them. They looked at us—the intruders on their mountain—then wandered away. We returned to the cabin and fell asleep to the gentle clomping of goat hooves on the rocky terrain outside.

Mountain goats also inhabit Mount Rushmore National Park in South Dakota, prompting some interesting ranger tales. Most of the thirty or so goats in the thirteen hundred-acre park browse in undergrowth behind the famous granite sculptures of George Washington, Thomas Jefferson, Abraham Lincoln, and Theodore Roosevelt. Occasionally some appear on the talus slopes of rock or even on the massive sculptures themselves.

Visitors are always delighted to see the goats and park interpreters learn to incorporate them into their lectures. Ranger discourses on the history of the site and the sculptures are often interrupted by goats picking their way across Abraham Lincoln's beard.

"They're a tough act to follow," smiled Interpretive Ranger Ernest Davis. "You're trying hard to tell people about sculptor Gutzon Borglum and how he spent fourteen years carving these huge sculptures and there are the mountain goats up there on the rocks, drawing everyone's attention. We find we have to quickly include something about the goats in our talk."

In addition to Glacier and Mount Rushmore, mountain goats might also be found at Mount Rainier National Park, North Cascades National Park, and Olympic National Park, all in Washington state.

Grizzly Bear

Ranger Mike Wacker has not seen many grizzly bears during his summers at Glacier National Park, but the few encounters he's had are vividly etched in his memory.

It was early one evening when he and a friend were on the homeward leg of a cross-country hike into the wild, western portion of the park. All at once the pair heard a thrashing in the underbrush about fifty yards ahead of them. At first they saw nothing. But then they caught the silvery glint of the coat and the hulking form of a grizzly crashing through the forest, running full throttle away from them.

"We obviously had surprised it as it was sleeping in a thicket or feeding," Mike recalled. "I'm sure it smelled us or heard us coming before we saw or heard it. But that's the way most people will see a bear—when they least expect it!"

The incident underscores a characteristic of the grizzly. Although it is the largest and strongest carnivore in the wilderness, the grizzly is not anxious to cross

grizzly bear

paths with humans. These big animals like a lot of space and are not tolerant of those who intrude on it.

Today, grizzlies are found in only a few areas in the lower forty-eight states: along the Continental Divide of the Rocky Mountains in northern Montana and Idaho; in a region that has Glacier National Park at its center; in the northwestern part of Wyoming in the Yellowstone ecosystem; and in the Cascade Range of northern Washington.

An estimated eight hundred grizzlies live in these three regions. Additional thousands inhabit western Canada and Alaska.

Officials at Yellowstone National Park took a big step toward keeping grizzlies away from people in the late 1960s when they eliminated the garbage dumps where leftover food had lured the bears close to visitors. Now the grizzlies that roam the Yellowstone ecosystem live naturally, as wild creatures in a wild world. "The grizzlies have to earn their own living in the backcountry," was the way Doug Scott, a wildlife biologist technician, put it.

What this means is that your chance of seeing a grizzly at either Glacier or Yellowstone is as remote as the bears.

A grizzly will cover a considerable distance while it feeds—as much as twenty or thirty miles. A bear's normal feeding range may include up to three hundred square miles, depending on the food available. Although ranges of individual bears do overlap, the bears keep themselves spread well apart.

The grizzly is not ordinarily a hunter that tracks and pursues its intended victim. Although it prefers the high protein content of meat, it is more likely to eat the flesh of an animal that it finds already dead (carrion). In many places, however, biologists have found that as much as ninety percent of its diet consists of vegetation.

The grizzly will eat almost anything and spends most of its waking hours wandering in search of food. It selects its feeding area according to the season of the year. In spring, valleys provide it with winter-killed elk or deer. Later the same places offer favorite fruits such as huckleberry, chokecherry, serviceberry, and currants. Along the shores of a lake or river a bear can snag a fish with its paw or feast on lush shore vegetation. High meadows and rocky mountain slopes provide grasses, roots, and small mammals such as ground squirrels and marmots. All of these seasonal feeding grounds must be available for a grizzly bear to thrive.

The grizzly is quite different from the black bear that also inhabits both the Glacier and Yellowstone wilderness. The grizzly is usually about twice the size of a black bear and varies in color from black brown to straw yellow. The grizzly weighs from 325 to 850 pounds or more, while the black bear weighs from 200 to 475 pounds. The grizzly's coat, as its name implies, is "grizzled-looking," the tips of its hair are silvery. The black bear's coat is glossy black or brown.

The characteristic that most sets the grizzly apart from the black bear, however, is the muscular hump over its front shoulders and its concave or "scooped-out" nose; a black bear's snout is long and tapered.

A grizzly's claws are longer and straighter than those of a black bear, equipping it to dig up sod and earth to get at roots, bulbs, and rodents, or to tear apart a rotting log to eat the ants beneath. The track of a grizzly usually displays these long claw marks as part of the footprint.

Grizzlies generally lead a solitary life, although several may be seen together if they discover a rich supply of acorns or fish. The animal may be active at any time of the day or night but often will bed down to rest during the middle of the day.

Male and female grizzlies pair up for several weeks during the breeding season of May through July, but both sexes may also mate with other individuals. A process called delayed implantation in the sow bear postpones development and delays the birth of her cubs until the following January or February when she is safely in her winter den.

Perhaps during the summer months when a bear would not be in residence, a ranger might show you a den. It is often located on the slope of a hill, usually on the north side to insure that a deep, insulating blanket of snow piles up in front of it. A favorite location is under the roots of a large tree, where the roots serve as a sort of ceiling support for the top of the den. Bears will pull evergreen branches into the den to make a cozy hideaway for their long winter sleep.

Bears often enter their dens during the first heavy snow of winter when their tracks into the den will be obliterated by snow, making it impossible for other animals to track the bear to its hiding place. A bear actually "estivates," rather than hibernates. Its body temperature drops very little and its metabolic rate remains comparatively high. In addition, it may arouse itself and venture out to forage for food if the weather is mild rather than sleep away the entire winter in a deep sleep, as some rodents do.

The mother bear gives birth in the den to her cubs, usually twins, which are only about eighteen inches long, nearly hairless, and utterly helpless. Biologists have discovered that grizzlies produce more males than females. Out of one hundred births, fifty-nine are male and forty-one female. But by the time the animals are four or five years old, the survival ratio becomes even.

A grizzly takes a long time to grow up from a hairless newborn; it needs five or six years to attain adult size. Like all young, bear cubs are voracious feeders, pausing often in their playing, fighting, and rambling to nurse from their mothers. A cub hums contentedly while nursing, much the way a kitten purrs.

Grizzly cubs stay with their mothers for at least two winters and many remain for an extra year. This provides them with more guidance on surviving in the wild—a useful apprenticeship to becoming an adult bear.

By the time a grizzly is three to four years old, it is ready to venture out on its own. It is a subadult bear now—an awkward period akin to the human teenage years. A young male bear, or boar, weighs some two hundred and fifty pounds at this age, a young sow a bit less. The young bear must find a territory to call its own. It does so by wandering around until it finds a locale that provides an ample food supply and a den location not already occupied by an adult bear.

One of the concerns of the Interagency Grizzly Bear Committee, a federal-state group organized to keep the grizzly bear, currently a threatened species, from becoming endangered, is the low reproductive rate of the bears. Since the animals produce an average of only one cub per adult female every two years, replacing bears that die or are killed is a slow process. The committee has recommended a bear recovery plan to coordinate all federal and state efforts to keep alive this symbol of the wilderness in its last strongholds.

Bighorn Sheep

The car ahead of us pulled off the tour road at the National Bison Range in Montana; its occupants motioned us to do the same. Pulling in behind their car, we realized what they were excitedly pointing out.

In front of us, fifty feet down the slope, lay three bighorn sheep—a ram, a ewe, and a young sheep, perhaps a yearling. Like many hoofed animals in the middle of the day, the sheep were resting quietly, digesting food they had eaten that morning. We noted how their gray brown coats blended with the earth and the tan grassland.

The ram's horns, massive compared to its body, completed a half-circle alongside its head. These horns continue to grow throughout a ram's life. In an older ram the horns may complete almost a full circle and can actually get in the way of the animal's vision.

Such horns can weigh as much as thirty pounds, as heavy as all the bones in a sheep's body. The larger the horns, the more dominant their owner. You can determine the age of a ram from the annual rings on its horns, just as you can with the mountain goat. The ewe has horns as well, but hers are smaller and have less curvature than the ram's.

We felt privileged to see these magnificent animals. They are the remaining few of throngs of bighorns that

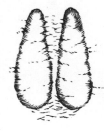

bighorn sheep

inhabited the mountain West until the late nineteenth century, when domestic cattle and sheep ranchers converted much of the prairie into grazing land for livestock. Disease, unlimited hunting, and overgrazing by livestock effectively pushed the bighorn sheep back into a few preserves in the northern Rockies. Another species, the desert bighorn sheep, inhabits the hot, dry, rocky cliffs and mountain regions of the Southwest.

The number of bighorns has continued to shrink; only an estimated twenty thousand survive within the United States today. Notable herds roam the mountain slopes of Glacier and Yellowstone national parks.

Another reason for the decline of the bighorn sheep is its migration habits. Young bighorns do not disperse and colonize new areas as do white-tailed deer, moose, and bears. Young bighorns follow in the footsteps of their parents, migrating year after year from summer feeding grounds in high mountain tundra to winter grazing grounds in the foothills. The youngsters learn this migration route as they grow up and do not vary from it. For this reason, efforts to transplant bighorn sheep from one location to an unpopulated area often are unsuccessful; the animals are unable to learn a new migration route.

The bighorn is a heavy-bodied animal (an adult male weighs from 125 to 275 pounds) with a two-layer coat that keeps it warm on mountain heights. An outer coat

Two young bighorn sheep roam the rocky terrain. If threatened, the sheep escape by climbing to heights where predators cannot follow.

of brittle guard hairs overlays a thick underfur, or fleece. A distinctive white patch on its rump, together with the spiral horns, will help you identify this animal.

The bighorn has excellent eyesight. Rangers say it is almost impossible to approach a bighorn without being seen. It also has a remarkable capacity for climbing and jumping from rock to rock, thanks to the structure of its hooves. The halves of each hoof separate so that the feet can cling firmly to the rockiest terrain. Soles of the feet are soft and cushionlike, allowing the bighorn to keep its balance as it moves across uneven or slippery surfaces.

These sheep are relatively invulnerable to predators because of their ability to escape into the heights. But when migrating, they descend to the foothills where their sure-footedness gives them no special advantage. Then they may fall prey to mountain lions or other large predators.

In spring and summer the bighorn is primarily a grazer, eating plenty of grasses, sedges, and other herbs that grow in alpine meadows, building up body fat for winter. Then, when plants are dormant or covered with snow, the sheep is reduced to browsing on forbs, shrubs, and trees such as sage, Douglas fir, willow, bearberry, rose, and mountain mahogany. It gets water from mountain pools or by eating snow.

When early November brings snow and cold to the higher elevations, bighorns begin their annual migration to their traditional breeding grounds at the lower elevations. As bands of males come together, social hierarchies mix; rams battle to establish or maintain their rank.

Among the episodes of animal behavior that wildlife watchers might witness, few can surpass the thrill of watching two rams go head-to-head as they fight it out to see who will be king of the mountain. Two rivals rear on their hind legs, then drop to all fours, slamming together head-on with a crack of horns that can be heard a mile away. The shock wave ripples through their bodies. Recovering, each stands still for as long as a minute to show off its horns to the other.

Again and again each of these determined antagonists puts its full weight behind a charge and clashes with the other. Chips may fly from horns and blood might ooze from an ear or nose. Finally, one of the battlers, exhausted or injured, behaves in a subordinate manner by lowering its head. The winner marches away to claim several ewes as its prize.

A thick facial hide and a porous, double-layered skull cushion the combatants during such head-on fights. Even so, both victor and vanquished earn the nose scars and blunted horns you see on veteran bighorn battlers.

After the herd migrates back to the high country, spring ushers in the lambing season. An expectant ewe slips away from the herd and climbs to a sheltered ledge to bear her young, usually a single lamb. In only a few hours the baby sheep can stand on wobbly legs to nurse from its mother, who also may be keeping watch for a hovering golden eagle, which can capture a baby lamb in the same way it snatches a baby mountain goat.

Soon the ewe leads her newborn to a nursery set among craggy rocks where her lamb and others will be safer from predators. Here they learn to nibble their first tender foliage, nursing less often. After staying in the nursery for about a month, mother and lamb rejoin the herd grazing in the alpine meadows.

Elk (Wapiti)

elk

On a September evening at Rocky Mountain National Park in Colorado we discovered that watching wildlife can even be a spectator sport.

We wanted to get a good vantage point from which to observe the elk; we had been told they would come at dusk to graze in the Horseshoe Park area. So we arrived early and found a parking spot along the park tour road.

In the next half-hour we counted 150 people in cars, vans, pickup trucks, trailers, and motorcycles. They parked bumper to bumper on the shoulder of the road like fans streaming in for a football game. Out came binoculars, spotting scopes, tape recorders, and long camera lenses to document the elk behavior. Out also came folding lawn chairs, thermos bottles, picnic bags, and blankets to keep the observers fortified against the chilly evening air while they waited to view the animals.

Everyone seemed to know that this was one of the prime feeding meadows for elk during the mating season, or rut. They had come simply to observe these sleek animals, to watch their social interaction, and to hear a bull give his splendid bugle call.

While we waited we fell into conversation with other elk enthusiasts, including Steve and Debbie Decker, a young couple who had driven forty miles from Boulder after work to watch the elk. Based on Steve's experience observing the rut in other years, he explained some of the elk behavior we would see: how a bull elk at this season of the year gathers a harem of cows, how he must be constantly vigilant to prevent another aggressive bull from cutting in on his harem, and how he will drive away even a yearling male (called a "spike" because of his single-tine antler) who may want only to be with his mother.

As dusk came to the meadow, a murmur passed along the line of spectators. Binoculars were raised. We took a look too. Far across the grassy expanse a single cow emerged from the surrounding forest and meandered into the meadow. A few minutes later another cow came, and then another.

Steve interpreted the unfolding scene. "Watch for other cows to come out, then finally the bull," he said. "The bull is checking for safety by sending a cow into the clearing first. She would become the target for any hunter or a predator who was lying in wait. Only when the bull feels the coast is clear will he step out!"

Sure enough. Nine cows grazed their way into the meadow before the bull elk put in his appearance, his head crowned with an impressive rack of antlers. It was too dark to count their points. A bull four or more years old may have a rack with six or more points. When a bull reaches seven points, wildlife observers call it a "royal." If it bears eight points, it is a "monarch."

Slowly the herd moved across the meadow, through a windbreak of trees and shrubs to an adjacent meadow. We watched through our binoculars in the gathering darkness. We were disappointed to hear no bugling— Steve said that evidently this bull did not want to challenge other bulls in the area, and no other bulls came to challenge him.

A bull elk, we learned later at a ranger talk, bugles for several reasons. Bugling relieves frustrations the bull builds up patrolling the perimeter of his harem to keep the cows from straying. It also serves as a warning to other bulls to keep their distance.

Finally, a bull bellows in the hope that the bugle's depth and tone will intimidate any potential rival, allowing the keeper of the harem to avoid a direct confrontation with the contending male. The unforgettable bugle starts with a low coarse bellow, rises to a clear high tone, then explodes in a series of grunts: *a-a-a-eeee-uuuuh! e-ugh! e-ugh! e-ugh!*

By now it was almost dark and the herd faded into the gloom. Car headlights flicked on and people folded their chairs, departing like spectators after an athletic event. Auto lights traced the road out of the valley. Elk watching had ended until the next night.

The elk is the second largest member of the deer family, after the moose. Its light, gray brown coat, together with its large yellowish rump patch and dark brown head and neck, earned it the Indian name *wapiti*, or white deer. European settlers mistakenly called it an elk, from the German word *elch*, which refers to the European moose. As a result, said one authority, the animal has been "saddled with a name that is harder to shed than a male's antlers."

You can see large herds of elk not only at Rocky Mountain National Park but also at Glacier National Park, Olympic National Park, Yellowstone National Park, Grand Teton National Park, the National Elk Refuge, and in smaller numbers in several Midwestern and Eastern states.

One of the last great animal migrations on the continent takes place in Wyoming in late October or early

Elk graze through desert vegetation at Yellowstone National Park. Like most members of the deer family, elk are both grazers and browsers.

November, when the first heavy snowfalls in the Rockies prompt the descent of bands of elk to their winter range around Jackson Hole, following a well-defined migration route. Along the way the bands merge into sizable herds.

In these rugged reaches of the Rockies, man has encroached on the wapiti's natural wintering grounds— the valley bottoms and foothill country where the snowfall is light enough for the elk to reach the cured grasses beneath. Settlers have fenced in fields, stocked the land with cattle, and harvested hay for domestic livestock. Caught between the snow-locked mountains and the privately owned valleys, many elk starved to death in years past.

Today parks and wildlife preserves as well as winter feedings help provide for the herds, notably at the National Elk Refuge in Jackson. The refuge was established by Congress in 1912 to provide a winter range for elk after thousands of the animals died in heavy snows in preceding years. Other lands were added to the refuge later, including 1,760 acres donated by the Izaak Walton League of America. It currently includes 24,700 acres that provide winter grazing for some eight thousand elk each winter.

On the balmy September day Assistant Refuge Manager Jim Griffin showed us around, we tried to imagine the brown herds that populate the preserve each winter. Once the elk arrive, he said, they stay until about May, when the herd migrates back to the high country in Grand Teton and Yellowstone parks and the surrounding national forests. In addition to protecting the elk, he pointed out, the refuge provides a sanctuary for other animals as well, including seldom seen but endangered species such as the whooping crane, peregrine falcon, and bald eagle.

Jim took us to the cabin that serves as a visitor's center where refuge guides bring school groups. At a "Touch-Feel" table students handle an elk's antlers (either bare or in velvet), skulls, fur, droppings, and the alfalfa pellets the refuge feeds to elk when necessary to help them survive the deep snows of winter.

Should you visit the National Elk Refuge during winter you may climb aboard a wooden sleigh drawn by a team of draft horses and experience a wildlife excursion as the driver guides you through scattered clusters of elk that fill the wide, flat grounds. The sleigh pulls you to within a few feet of these regal animals—calves, cows, spike bulls, and mature males topped with great racks of antlers that spread some four or five feet across.

A bull elk, Jim said, loses his antlers in late winter. When spring comes, the large herds break up and scatter when the elk drift up the valleys to high country. The bulls then wander off alone or in small groups to grow new antlers and fatten on the alpine meadows.

Summer forage includes grasses, sedges, broadleafed herbs, and mushrooms. In winter elk dig through snow with their sharp hooves to reach grass and browse above the snow line on twigs, bark, and buds of deciduous trees such as aspen, willow, mountain maple, and chokecherry.

It is easy to see where elk have made a feast of a grove of aspen trees. Wherever you go in elk country, black scars and "browse lines" are evident on the whitish bark of the aspens. Look closely at an elk-scarred tree. Notice how the animal scrapes off the bark with an upward motion rather than downward. This is because an elk has incisors only in its lower jaw; its upper jaw has a hard pad instead of incisors. Its teeth are well-adapted to shredding off twigs and nipping grass, but not to scraping bark downward.

Once back on the upper slopes in spring, it is time for the cows to give birth, usually in early June, to a single calf with a tan coat with white spots. Mother and calf live alone for the first twenty days, the youngster well hidden under cover. The calf can stand up within hours of its birth. In a day it gains the strength to follow its mother. Grazing begins at four weeks but the calf continues to nurse until at least three months of age, when it loses its spots and grows its brown winter coat.

Elk are one of the most abundant animals in parks such as Yellowstone and Rocky Mountain. They are readily seen. At Yellowstone they wander through campgrounds and onto the lawns surrounding park buildings. More than once we had to slow our motor home to allow an elk to mosey across the road to see if the grass was greener on the other side.

"They become habituated to people," said Yellowstone's Doug Scott, "but they are still wild animals. If a careless visitor gets closer than about ten feet an elk will just move away. I can't remember the last time anyone was injured by one. But we advise visitors to stay about a hundred feet away so as not to disturb the animals."

The old instincts remain. Even though they are accustomed to people, Doug said, elk cows still retreat from the park and go into the hills to have their calves.

Mountain Lion

This tawny, powerful, secretive cat is known by different names in different sections of the country. It is a mountain lion, cougar, puma, panther, painter, or catamount (a "cat of the mountains"). But no matter what you call it, it is unlikely you will see one—for at least two reasons.

First, relatively few mountain lions remain in much of the mountain backcountry, even though a century ago this big cat had the widest distribution of any single species of mammal in the country. But livestock owners, bounty hunters, and sportsmen reduced its numbers until today mountain lions are found only in the most rugged mountain areas of the western and southwestern states. Perhaps forty-five to sixty-five hundred mountain lions prowl the wilderness areas. Its cousin, the Florida panther, has dwindled in numbers to only a few in the southern reaches of the Florida peninsula (see page 90).

Second, this sleek, nocturnal predator makes its living by being secretive, remaining hidden from its prey until the moment it pounces, and by staying out of man's way. With its tan hide, it blends in with surroundings as it moves through the forest and rocky slopes. A number of rangers who have served for years at Glacier and Yellowstone, where mountain lions are known to live, have never seen one.

mountain lion

The mountain lion is built to be a predator. With its narrow, muscular torso and large padded feet, it stalks quietly after prey such as deer or elk. Since its forelimbs are heavier and shorter than its hind legs, the animal walks with its hindquarters held higher than the rest of its body. It is capable of incredible physical feats: it can cover forty-five feet in a single bound, leap eighteen feet into a tree, and race over even rough terrain smoothly and swiftly, balancing itself by swinging its long, heavy tail from side to side.

Its sharp eyes permit it to see its quarry in almost total darkness; its eyes can pick up an object in light six times dimmer than that which man needs to see. Therefore, much of its hunting is at night. At a twitch of its muscles, its claws extend from the soft padding of its feet. There are five claws on each forefoot, four on each hindfoot.

Predators like the mountain lion help preserve the balance of nature by keeping in check the increasing populations of deer and elk. In addition, the mountain lion goes after porcupines, skunks, beavers, and rabbits. After killing a large animal, the lion gorges itself until it is full, then pulls the remaining carcass to a secluded spot and covers it with leaves and grass to be consumed at another time.

A mountain lion patrols a territory that varies from five to twenty-five square miles for a female and fifteen to thirty square miles for a male. Sometimes the ranges of several lions overlap, but they avoid each other by leaving a sign called a "scrape." The animal scrapes together leaves, twigs, and pine needles into a pile four to six inches high, then urinates on it as a way of notifying other lions of its presence. It leaves its scrape in spots where traffic is heaviest—under a tree, on a ridge, at the crossroads of two hunting trails.

Maurice Hornocker, a biologist at the University of Idaho who tracked mountain lions in the Idaho wilderness, concluded that mutual avoidance was important to the preservation of the mountain lion as a species.

"Because they are solitary predators," Hornocker wrote, "lions have to depend on their physical well-being, their agility, to survive; consequently, fighting in defense of their territory, as do some gregarious species such as wolves, is a luxury lions cannot afford. An injured wolf may survive because he is a member of the pack; an injured solitary lion most likely would starve."

At mating time a lion screams loudly to attract a lioness; this mating call is undoubtedly the explanation of numerous reports from people who have heard blood-curdling screams in the forest. After mating, the two lions go their separate ways once more.

For her den the female selects an isolated cave or sheltered ledge. Here she bears one to five spotted cubs—usually in late winter or early spring, three months after mating.

Until they are several months old, the kittens feed only on their mother's milk. When the young ones first venture outside the den, their mother brings them bones and meat. Soon the offspring accompany her on hunting forays and she teaches them to stalk and run down game. They may stay with their mother for as long as two years before heading off to establish a home range of their own. Meanwhile, the father lives and hunts alone, except during the brief mating period.

Beaver

beaver

Marge and I had been fortunate to see beavers hard at work during a ranger walk at Grand Teton National Park. Later, at Rocky Mountain National Park, we observed a dramatic example of the effect a beaver's actions can have on the landscape.

Walking along the Fern Lake Trail, we came across a grove of aspen trees that had been literally "clear cut" by beavers. Almost every tree, all of which were three to five inches in diameter, had been brought down. The stumps showed the cone-shaped cuts and chisel marks made by the sharp incisor teeth of these aquatic lumberjacks.

As we explored the area we noticed logs the beavers had cut into manageable lengths, skid marks where they had laboriously dragged the logs to the riverbank, and a slide where these clever workers had slid the logs into a stream to float them to a pond to build their dam and lodge.

To cut and fell a tree, a beaver uses its four large, curved incisor teeth. These teeth are bright orange, grow throughout the animal's life, and are self-sharpening. Thus equipped, a beaver can cut through a tree trunk with surprising speed.

Standing on its hind legs and balancing itself with its large tail, the beaver turns its head sideways and anchors its upper teeth into the tree. By bringing up its lower teeth and twisting its head, it tears out a large chip. Working around the tree, it makes a deeper and wider cut until the tree topples.

The old story that a beaver can control the direction in which a tree falls is a myth, rangers told us. Instead, the tree falls toward the side with the heaviest branches. Very often, however, the side where sunlight has produced the heaviest branches is the side toward the pond.

A beaver may not be able to control the fall of a tree, but it does exert a surprising amount of control over its own environment. Most animals must find themselves a habitat that is suitable to live in; the beaver actually alters a landscape and fashions a habitat to suit itself. At the same time it starts a chain of events that affects other wildlife as well.

We saw an example when we drove Trail Ridge Road, which traverses Rocky Mountain park. Downslope from the road, in a valley where a stream flowed, beavers had created a series of dams and ponds, which had slowed the flow of the stream and changed the landscape to look like a terrace of oriental rice paddies.

Other changes would follow. A pond that backs up behind a beaver dam covers the bases of the trees growing there, causing them to die. The ponds often attract wildlife such as fish, ducks, waterbirds, and amphibians. Otters, raccoons, ospreys, hawks, owls, and other predators will be next to arrive, attracted by the new possibilities for prey.

After the beavers exhaust the supply of food in an area—and this may take ten years or more—they move on. The dam usually remains intact for several more years, accumulating silt and leaves. Finally, during a spring thaw or a long, hard rain, the dam gives way. The pond water drains away, leaving an open area where grass, shrubs, and berry bushes grow. Insects and small rodents thrive, attracting deer, bear, grouse, and other animals as a new habitat evolves from what the beavers started.

The beaver is the largest rodent in the United States and is found throughout the country, except in the desert Southwest. It has short legs, webbed hindfeet, and a flat, scaly tail that serves as a brace when it stands. The beaver slaps its tail on the water's surface as a danger signal to other beavers should a predator approach.

The beaver is an accomplished engineer, using its sharp teeth, webbed feet, and tail as tools. After cutting and hauling logs to a site, it constructs the dam's base out of logs and nearby stones, then wedges the ends of sticks under the rocks, with their free ends leaning in the direction of the current. After weaving a latticework of brush around the sticks, the beaver scoops mud from the stream bed and plasters it against the dam face. Sediment and debris carried downstream fills in the chinks.

Once the dam is built and a pool created that is deep enough to avoid freezing in winter, the beaver constructs a lodge, usually in the middle of the pond where the family will be safe from predators.

The lodge is probably the first thing you see in beaver country—a large conical pile of logs, sticks, brush, and mud often about six feet high. A beaver lodge usually has two underwater entrances; inside, a dry chamber above water level is used for socializing, grooming, and sleeping. Beavers who live along turbulent streams that flow too fast to dam build their lodge at the water's edge and burrow into the stream bank.

Near its lodge the beaver stacks a mass of branches and sticks underwater—its food supply for the winter. Even when the pond is sealed by winter ice, the beaver stays snug and warm in its shelter of sticks and mud plaster. When hungry, it slips out through its underwater entrance and swims beneath the surface, selecting a tasty branch from its submerged food supply. It also nibbles aquatic plants that grow on the pond's bottom. A beaver can stay underwater for some fifteen minutes at a time and sometimes even finds bubbles of air under the ice to breathe.

Long guard hairs, which flatten when wet, shield its fine underfur. Oil secreted from two large glands under its tail waterproofs its coat. To groom itself, the beaver uses its two hindfeet to apply the oil.

The female gives birth to three or four kits in the lodge, usually in April or May. At that time the father and any two-year-olds still living at home depart to establish a new residence elsewhere, leaving the lodge to the mother and her young.

Kits weigh about one pound at birth and are covered with fur. Each newborn can walk almost immediately and soon learns to swim. At year's end the youngster is half grown; at two years of age it is ready to mate and establish a lodge of its own.

Beavers are social creatures, typically found in a family colony consisting of a dominant female, an adult male, several yearlings, and three or four kits. They are normally active at dusk, during the night, and at dawn, but it is not unusual to see them out on a cloudy day or even sunning themselves on a warm day.

Rangers say the best time to look for beavers is at dusk when they emerge from their lodge to begin a night's work, forage for plants, or waddle ashore to cut some trees. Ask at the park visitor center for locations where beavers are known to be active. Then find a quiet, hidden spot and watch for these master builders at nightfall.

Marmot

You will almost always hear a marmot before you see it. The first leg of the trail to Sperry Glacier, high in the mountains at Glacier National Park, led us through rocky terrain past several large boulders. A series of shrill whistles sounded from the midst of the boulders. A marmot—the customary sentinel marmot—sat atop a huge rock looking directly at us, transmitting its warning to its compatriots.

With a high-pitched squeak, another marmot gave us a quick scolding for invading its territory, then scampered down into the rocks. As we continued up the trail the sentinel marmot dropped to all fours from its "on-guard" sitting position, then darted to the far side of the boulder and out of sight. When we walked by the spot a moment or two later not a marmot was visible or audible.

The marmot, the heavyweight of the ground squirrel family, makes its home in high mountains, particularly in rock slides (talus slopes), lava beds, and alpine meadows. Many of its actions reminded us of its smaller fellow rodent, the prairie dog of the plains.

Marmots will probably keep you company wherever you hike in the high Rocky or Cascade mountains. The

marmot

hoary marmot is found at altitudes of up to twelve thousand feet throughout the northwestern states and Canada and Alaska. It is grizzled gray in color, and has black feet and black and white markings on its head.

The yellow-bellied marmot, the second most common variety, is found throughout the Rocky, Sierra Nevada, and Cascade mountains and south as far as California, Nevada, Utah, and Colorado. It is brown with a yellowish tinge to its coat and has distinctive black and white markings on its head.

The marmot is the western cousin of the woodchuck of the East. In fact, most Westerners call it a "rockchuck," an apt term since the animal makes its home beneath the rock piles that protect it from predators such as the bear, coyote, wolf, fox, and golden eagle.

A marmot is not a small animal. It is twice the size of a prairie dog and about five times as heavy, weighing from eight to fifteen pounds. Early French trappers called it *le siffleur*, "the whistler." Marmots also bark and hiss.

A typical marmot colony contains a breeding male, three to five adult females, and up to twenty young. The youngsters include yearlings as well as juveniles in their first summer. Family members forage a territory of an acre or two of alpine meadow that lies adjacent to their rocky home. Territories are usually on the south slope of a mountain and up near timberline.

A marmot fattens up all summer on a diet of sedges, lichens, roots, berries, and grasses, sometimes growing so fat that its belly drags on the ground. After a big meal it may stretch out on a warm rock or retreat to its burrow to take a snooze.

The marmot is a true hibernator. In late August or early September it heads for its grassy bed deep within the rocks, there to fall into a remarkable deep sleep that will last until the following May. The marmot's body temperature, biologists calculate, drops to thirty-six degrees Fahrenheit, its respiration slows to one breath every five minutes, and its heart rate drops to five beats per minute.

Finally roused from its long sleep in the spring, the marmot mates. Five weeks later, litters of two to five little ones are born in the den. The young remain with their mother throughout summer and stay with the family until the middle of their second summer, when they are experienced enough to face their alpine world alone.

If you can find a good observation place near a marmot colony, you will enjoy watching the social interactions of these mountain rodents. Young marmots, like young prairie dogs, grapple and wrestle, pouncing on each other and darting about. Such playful tactics, biologists believe, help the young marmot learn where it fits into the hierarchy of marmot society.

Rangers can tell you some odd stories of marmot playfulness. At one park a woman put her camera on the ground for a minute; a marmot seized it in its teeth and ran off. Only when she gave chase did the rodent drop its stolen prize and head for the rocks.

At Glacier National Park a ranger left his car door open as he talked with a group of visitors. When he got back to park headquarters he realized that a marmot had hopped into the car when he was not looking and had hitchhiked a ride to headquarters.

Pika

If the marmot knows how to relax, another creature of the high alpine mountain regions is devoted to hard work. This gray brown animal, which looks like a guinea pig in a fur coat, also inhabits the rock slides and talus slopes of the western mountains.

To observe the pika in its native habitat we took an aerial tram ride to the windy summit of Rendezvous Peak, west of Grand Teton National Park. Here we met Larry Livingood, a former teacher who serves as staff naturalist for the Jackson Hole Ski Corporation. In summer Larry provides wildlife information to visitors like us; in winter he functions as a member of the resort's avalanche forecasting team.

With Larry in the lead we picked our way over the jumbled limestone slope, buffeted by a forty-five-mile-an-hour wind. During a lull we heard an *eek-eek-eek* and spied a pika, its color blending with the rocks as it scampered across a slab. After Larry left us, we pulled our lunch from our trail packs and sat down to study this little mountaineer.

In a few minutes, when the pika had become accustomed to our presence, it emerged from a crevice and trotted across a patch of vegetation, continuing to emit its high-pitched squeak. Returning with a mouthful of grass and flowers, it deposited them on top of the heap of vegetation it was collecting in a nearby cranny.

pika

The pika, we learned, makes hay while the sun shines. It stacks up a pile of grass, sedges, and flowers in the sun to dry. After the sunlight cures the vegetation into "hay," the pika gathers load after load and carries it into its burrow beneath the rocks, where it will provide a winter food supply when snow blankets the mountains.

Should rain fall, the pika bustles about getting its crop under cover, much as human farmers on the prairie do at this season of the year. Each owner jealously guards its own pile, chasing off intruding pikas and marking each of its stacks with urine and with the scent from a facial gland. By summer's end each pika may boast a fifty-pound hay mow—150 times its own weight—to feed on in the cold months ahead.

When the snows fly the pika retreats to this well-provisioned home below ground. Here it lives in a system of interconnecting gaps between the rocks. This

maze of natural passages discourages a weasel from trying to follow the rodent and gives the pika protection
from its other major enemy, the hawks that patrol the
mountain skies. Larry once measured the temperature of
a pika's winter home a foot or so beneath the surface
and found it to be a comfortable forty-five degrees
Fahrenheit.

A roundish body, short legs, and dense fur conserve
the pika's body heat. The soles of its feet are fur-clad—for
warmth and for traction on slippery rocks. It has two
extra incisor teeth in its upper jaw, a feature that indicates the pika's relation to the rabbit. Consequently,
many Westerners call it a "rockrabbit."

The busy rodent does not stray far from its well-
concealed home. It marks off its front and back yards as
its territory, posting "No Trespassing" signs by rubbing its
scent against rocks or plants and by constantly chirping
to announce its presence. If it discovers another rockrabbit in its backyard, it will give chase and nip the
offender until it retreats.

Pikas work and live in solitude most of the year but,
like other animals, pair up briefly during the breeding
season. With pikas, mating occurs twice, once in spring
and again in summer. Females produce litters that average three babies apiece. The young are born in a nest
deep in the rocks and are able to crawl within hours.

They begin to nibble on green plants in two weeks
and may then be seen tumbling and playing near their
rocky entrance. Young pikas develop rapidly—nature's
way of fitting their life cycle to the short growing season
of the high mountains. After only thirty days the young
are driven away by their mothers to seek their own
territory.

Pikas are usually active in early morning or on
cloudy days when their bodies do not cast the dark
shadow that would be visible to a sharp-eyed hawk. You
can readily tell a pika from other common mountain
rodents such as the marmot, ground squirrel, and chipmunk. The marmot is about three times bigger. Both the
ground squirrel and the chipmunk have stripes on their
back as well as a bushy tail; the pika has little or no
visible tail.

Porcupine

Many a camper has crawled out of his tent in the morning to find a canoe handle, an axe, or his boots gnawed
and pitted by some animal. Later he discovers that the
culprit was a porcupine, an animal that craves salt so
much that it will eat even a perspiration-soaked paddle
or boot.

Its liking for salt is only one odd characteristic of the
porcupine, a wild animal like no other creature you will

porcupine

observe. The porcupine inhabits forested areas in most parts of the United States, except the Southeast.

There's nothing flashy about the porcupine. About two feet in length with a seven- to nine-inch tail, this blackish "pincushion of the forest" moves slowly on its short legs, laboriously climbing a tree by using its claws and the soft pads on its feet. This clumsy climber has poor eyesight, although its senses of smell and hearing are good.

These unexceptional characteristics might seem to make the porcupine an easy quarry for potential enemies. But any shortcomings are quickly neutralized by the porcupine's formidable defense mechanism—some thirty thousand quills interspersed among the hairs on its stubby body.

When attacked, the porcupine raises its quills, turns its back to its attacker, and covers its face with its front feet. Its feet stomping the ground like a skunk, its teeth chattering, and its tail lashing the air, it presents a frightening target.

An aggressor such as a fox, coyote, or bobcat will likely end up with a painful face or paw full of quills. The quills, controlled by a layer of muscle beneath its coat, detach easily from a porcupine's skin—but are not "shot" at a target as some folk tales suggest. New quills will soon grow in.

The barbed quills range from one-quarter inch to four inches in length. They stick into a predator's flesh and may bury themselves deeper and deeper until they puncture a vital organ, eventually bringing death to the attacker. These spines also absorb the body fluids of the attacker, resulting in swelling that makes them much harder to remove.

It is no wonder that most potential predators give the porcupine a wide berth. Only one seems to be able to attack it with consistent success. That is the fisher, a member of the weasel family that attacks from a low angle in front, using its quick reflexes to inflict wounds on the porcupine's face and flipping it over to expose its spineless underbelly.

In winter the porcupine seldom strays far from its favorite clump of trees, which include hemlock, spruce, pine, basswood, maple, beech, birch, and aspen. Its powerful incisor teeth, which look much like the beaver's, cut easily through a tree's tough outer bark to the nutritious inner layer of cambium. It munches away with a total of twenty teeth.

Although woody material that consists largely of cellulose is normally difficult for animals to digest, the porcupine can handle it. It has a long digestive tract in which special bacteria break down the cellulose into carbohydrates that nourish the porcupine—but give many a forester a headache as the gnawing animal destroys tree after tree.

In spring, summer, and fall the porcupine varies its diet with grasses and sedges, and the flowers, leaves, twigs, roots, catkins, and seeds of other plants.

Knowing the porcupine's eating habits makes it easier to observe this slow-moving forest dweller. Look for the destructive rectangular debarked areas the porcupine scrapes from tree trunks and for wood chips and droppings that have fallen around the base of the tree.

Come back the same evening at dusk or after dark with a flashlight and investigate the same tree, and those nearby. When a porcupine eats away at a tree trunk, the tree's sap coagulates at the wound to try to repair the damage. The porcupine returns to the damaged tree to gnaw farther into this sweet material. You may very well find the animal back feeding on the same tree that night. During the day the porcupine often rests, usually curled up in a furry ball where a branch meets the trunk of a tree, possibly in the same tree where he will dine that night.

Female porcupines give birth to a single pup in April, May, or June after a lengthy gestation of seven months. The baby porcupine weighs about a pound at birth. Its quills are about a quarter-inch long and are soft and hairlike, but they soon grow hard and functional as they dry. Within fifteen minutes of birth the newborn can walk and lash its tail. It climbs in several weeks and gives up nursing in a month or so. By autumn the young porcupine is ready to cut its family ties.

To obtain their quota of salt, porcupines gnaw on the antlers shed by deer, elk, and moose and are said even to relish the glue used in making plywood. One explanation for the dead porcupine you may see in the road in winter is that a porcupine picked up the scent of the salt used by road crews to melt winter snow, wandered out onto the road at night, and was hit trying to lick up the salt.

Porcupines are surprisingly vocal for such lethargic animals. Observers report hearing wails in the night, probably a male porcupine trying to locate a female during the mating season. Porcupines also grunt, groan, bark, and whine; their calls may carry up to a quarter of a mile.

Moose

It was early on an August afternoon when we drove along the park road in Yellowstone National Park. We were not expecting to see much wildlife because we had learned that the best observation times were in the cool of early morning and the quiet of early evening. Nevertheless, Marge had her binoculars at her eyes as I drove our motor home, Tortuga, slowly along.

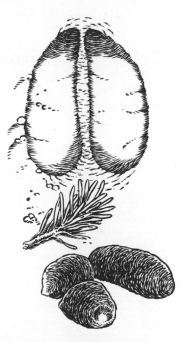

moose

"Slow down!" she said, with a note of excitement in her voice. "Pull over."

She peered intently into a dim glade just off the road, a shadowy retreat from the warm sun. A creek ran through it.

"It's a bull moose!" she exclaimed. Now the excitement was real. "Look at that rack of antlers!"

I grabbed my binoculars to see a big bull lying half hidden in the high grass near the stream, its broad, many-pointed antlers covered in velvet. Marge had been sharp-eyed indeed to have spotted only the animal's out-reaching antlers.

Another car pulled onto the shoulder behind us and a family got out to see what we had discovered. We pointed out the bull moose.

A few minutes later the mother in the family pointed her finger: "There's another one!"

We all looked where she was pointing and saw a second bull moose we had not seen before. No wonder. You could hardly see it in the high grass, even with its handsome set of antlers.

The two bulls lay placidly. They might not be so calm in another month when the rut would be in progress. At that time the bull moose's personality changes from docile to aggressive. His neck muscles swell and he becomes a "macho moose." He scrapes his antlers against rocks or trees and flourishes them as he threatens other bulls.

If he hears the grunting, mooing call of a cow, or another bull challenging his supremacy, a bull moose rumbles through the brush like a bulldozer, crashing into trees, shouldering his way through the undergrowth. If he meets a rival he lowers his head and makes an earth-shaking charge. Wielding their antlers, the two males try to outpush each other. The bull that establishes superiority gains the right to take several cows for his mates.

The moose is the largest member of the deer family, the group of animals that provides observers with such a varied segment of American wildlife. The moose is easy to recognize with its large size, dark to reddish brown color, humped back, and long muzzle. The bull wears large palmlike antlers that grow during the spring and summer, then fall off in the winter. The cow moose has no antlers.

In spite of its huge size (a full-grown bull weighs about a thousand pounds), a moose can run as fast as thirty-five miles an hour. When it runs it lifts each leg straight upward, making its gait almost comical. But the odd leg action serves a useful purpose: it allows the animal to lift its leg easily out of a muddy lake or stream bottom. The moose also has large dewclaws (vestigial hooves) on the rear of each hind leg, which may help keep the heavy animal from sinking too deeply into a muddy ooze.

Its legs are long, allowing the moose to stand in

shallow water to graze on aquatic plants and to move easily through even two-foot snowfalls. Its hooves are wide with pointed toes, leaving a heart-shaped track about 5½ inches long.

When it feeds in water, the moose shows no fear of putting its head underwater. It cherishes water lilies and will wade far out into a swampy pond, munching on plants on the surface or dipping its great head completely under the water to get at succulent roots.

A moose is a strong swimmer and has been known to dive underwater to yank up plants from the bottom. It can remain underwater for a full minute before resurfacing. Biologists have determined that a moose eats an average of 44 pounds of wet forage a day, but this amount increases to some 60 pounds in spring and an astounding 130 pounds daily in autumn.

After feasting on plant growth in a lake or swamp, a moose often leaves the water to find seclusion and relief from insect bites in a heavily wooded area. It browses on plants and trees such as willow, aspen, maple, and cherry, sometimes bending a sapling so it can nibble the tender upper leaves.

Moose calves, usually twins, are born in May and are dark brown. Unlike most other calves in the deer family, moose calves have no spots. The calves stay with their mother for a year, but she may drive them away the following spring, just before her new offspring arrive.

In the United States you have the opportunity to view moose only in the northern Rocky Mountains, the northern tier of states bordering the Great Lakes, and northern New England. Hundreds of thousands of moose, however, populate Canada and Alaska.

The national parks where moose can be seen are Glacier, Yellowstone, and, best of all, Grand Teton. In summer you will have a unique experience at Isle Royale National Park, a 210-square-mile wilderness island in Lake Superior. On this island, rangers will tell you, a wolf pack and a herd of several hundred moose coexist in a dynamic predator-prey relationship.

The moose, like all other animals of the western mountains, has its own niche within the wide range of environments in this region. This variety of habitat, in turn, is home to a panorama of species that offer unparalleled opportunities for outdoor observation.

CHAPTER 9

Wildlife of the Desert

We had driven for miles through the desert of the Southwest, crossing mostly brown and gray terrain dotted with the green of sagebrush, creosotebush, grama grass, and cactus. It was past six in the evening when we guided our motor home along a roller-coaster road through a former volcanic crater that defines the landscape of Tucson Mountain Park, a county park in southern Arizona.

Within a few minutes the scene changed dramatically. Giant saguaro cactuses raised their curving arms above the low-lying bushes. A late-summer rainstorm had just passed through, leaving the sparse desert vegetation glistening with raindrops and the road in front of us shining from the silvery reflection of the setting sun. On the horizon, not one, but three rainbows arched across the sky.

It was an appropriate introduction, we felt, to this region, which seems to offer either too much or too little of everything. Here, the highest temperature in the country has been recorded—134 degrees Fahrenheit at Death Valley. It is also here that temperatures at night can drop thirty to forty degrees below midday temperatures.

In the deserts of the Southwest it is so dry that the land receives an average of less than ten inches of precipitation a year. In some places there have been periods as long as two years without rain.

Yet when the infrequent rains do occur, they are likely to be downpours that accompany a thunderstorm, producing torrents of water that fill the *arroyos* (dry washes) and surge down gullies as flash floods that carry everything with them. Other streams channel the run-off water toward the sea—but it never gets there. Instead, streams flow into shallow lakes that have no outlets.

The deserts of the Southwest lie within the flat land basins stretching between the western slope of the

Rocky Mountains and the eastern slope of the Sierra Nevadas, extending through Nevada, Utah, southern California, Arizona, and New Mexico. The Great Basin, Mojave Desert, Sonoran Desert, and Chihuahuan Desert are the four major deserts of the region.

A desert, we learned, is no barren wasteland. It is made up of a variety of landforms resulting from its geologic history and years of erosion by rainwater run-off and wind. On this land grow plants that have adapted to the existing soil and to hot, dry conditions. The plants make efficient use of the little water they get. One of these adaptations is the "succulent," a plant such as the cactus that stores water within its thick stems, leaves, or roots. Its roots lie close to the surface of the ground, where they quickly absorb water from the occasional rains.

Other succulent plants have leaves that are thick and waxy, or thornlike, and therefore lose little water. Thus, these plants are able to store water for long periods and resist long dry spells.

The creosote bush, one of the most common desert plants, adapts by dropping some of its leaves in periods of drought. Other prevalent types of desert vegetation are sagebrush and saltbush; yucca, mesquite, and palo verde trees; and various cactuses such as the prickly pear, cholla, and organ pipe.

This sparse vegetation supports a surprising variety of wildlife. Like the plants, the animals of the desert need water to live and have developed specialized ways of obtaining and retaining it.

All desert animals, of course, soon find their way to any stream, spring, or seepage in their territory, but such surface water sources are scarce. Some animals, like the javelina, or wild pig, which eats a lot of prickly pear cactus, base their diets on succulents, obtaining water from juicy leaves. Desert-dwelling mice also get moisture from the prickly pear and can even climb up its sharp spines like a ladder. Predators get some moisture as well as protein from the meat they eat.

In addition, desert animals must conserve the water they get. Consequently, few large animals live in the desert; an animal with a large body surface would perspire too much or pant too heavily, thus losing a great deal of body fluid. The largest animals usually found in the desert are the mule deer, desert bighorn sheep, and coyote.

To conserve water, desert animals normally hunt and feed after sunset when the landscape cools off. Even coyotes, which hunt during the day in other regions, hunt at night in the desert. For the few animals that do venture out in daytime heat, water-saving strategy dictates that they occasionally seek the shade of rocks, bushes, or trees, like city people seeking refuge in one air-conditioned building after another.

On the other hand, lizards, snakes, and tortoises actually need warm temperatures because their cold-blooded bodies require it. But even these reptiles seek the shade when temperatures climb too high. Chuck-walla lizards warm up in the morning sun, then crawl into a shady spot at midday. A jackrabbit grazes on grass and plants but from time to time takes a "shade break" to cool off.

Some animals use another conservation technique: they use less water to eliminate their wastes. Jackrabbits, for example, leave behind very dry feces and discharge a more concentrated urine, thus saving their body's water supply.

Yet another water conservation action is to burrow underground. Ground squirrels, dashing about all day looking for seeds, occasionally return to their burrow. Even some birds seek shelter underground; the burrow-ing owl digs a tunnel up to ten feet long into a bank of earth to find relief from heat and protection from enemies.

We picked up some good tips on how to observe animals of the desert the day we visited Saguaro Na-tional Monument, a national park divided into two sec-tions: Saguaro West is twelve miles west of Tucson, Ari-zona, and Saguaro East lies fifteen miles to the east.

"The animals of the desert are smaller and better camouflaged than, for example, the animals of the Rockies," Seasonal Ranger Kimberly Otero explained to newcomers at the visitor center at Saguaro East. "So even if you are looking right at an animal, you might not see it unless it moved," she said. "Keep your eyes tuned to pick up any movement around you."

Time of day is even more critical for observing wild-life in the desert than in other regions, according to Bob Hall, the park's chief of resource management. "Most of the animals are either nocturnal or feed or hunt early in the morning or at dusk," he said. "Unfortunately, many of our visitors come to the park in the middle of the day, when the temperatures are the highest and the animals are the scarcest."

He emphasized the advice we had received else-where: the more you know about an animal's habitat the more likely you are to observe it.

"In this park," Bob said, "you should look carefully up and down the *arroyos* as you drive the loop roads." In the washes, he explained, are *tinajas* (Spanish for "tank" and pronounced tin-AH-hahz), pockets of water left by the last rainfall. Even in the hot summer some *tinajas* persist; animals use them as watering holes. Javelinas and other wildlife often forage for food around *tinajas*.

With this guidance firmly in mind, we were ready to get a closer look at the wildlife that lives in the demand-ing environment of the desert.

Kit Fox

Sure enough, as we drove the tour road at Saguaro National Monument late one afternoon, we spied a kit fox. The compact little animal trotted from behind a bush next to the road and quickly crossed, barely giving our vehicle a passing glance as it disappeared between several cactuses, probably intent on searching out dinner for that night.

The kit fox, the smallest of several types of foxes in North America, is about the size of a large house cat. It is rusty gray with white undersides and flaunts the fox's trademark, a bushy tail tipped in black. Its close relative is the desert swift fox.

Both are among the speediest of carnivores and can dash quickly for short distances to overtake prey. If surprised, the kit fox may flatten itself to the ground and lie still, hoping to escape notice. Threatened, it speeds away with its tail straight out behind, running with a smooth-flowing motion as effortless as a leaf in a breeze.

If pursued, it can wheel suddenly and take off in a new direction, throwing its pursuer off balance. If its burrow is close by, it heads for home and quickly dives into the burrow to avoid a predator such as a bobcat, coyote, or golden eagle.

kit fox

A distinctive characteristic that helps identify the kit fox is its large, triangular ears. They are its chief detection device, sensitive enough to pick up the slight rustle of a mouse in the sand. Its ears move independently, as do those of the mule deer, enabling it to listen for sounds coming from two directions.

On a hot day its ears act as a sort of radiator. A network of tiny capillaries in the ears circulates blood that becomes cooled in the air, keeping the fox's temperature down. Long, coarse hairs line the inside of each ear to keep desert dust from clogging the animal's efficient hearing apparatus.

The kit fox goes hunting for kangaroo rats, ground squirrels, and other small rodents, as well as jackrabbits, cottontail rabbits, and even ground-breeding birds, lizards, scorpions, bugs, and locusts. Once in a while it eats grass and cactus fruit.

It tries to catch its quarry unaware, stalking silently on feet covered with hair. Pouncing on its prey, it carries it back to the den to eat. Occasionally, it buries an uneaten portion near its den to eat later.

For its den the kit fox digs a tunnel into a sand dune or hillock, a narrow hole with two to five alternate exits for escape. In this shelter the fox sleeps during the heat of the day, dozing near the entrance where it can keep an alert eye on the neighborhood.

Unlike many other carnivores, the kit fox is willing to share its hunting territory of about one square mile with other foxes. It usually keeps to its territory, except during mating season when the male wanders afield in search of a female. When he finds her, he either moves in or makes a new den nearby.

Breeding takes place in late fall or early winter with the female usually giving birth to four or five pups in February or March. Both parents feed the young—the mother with her milk and the father with small rodents captured and brought back to the den.

By late summer the family separates and the pups venture off on their own. With luck, the young foxes find the prey they need and avoid predators as they make a new life for themselves in their desert environment.

Jackrabbit

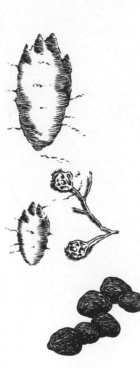

jackrabbit

When driving in the desert, it is not unusual to flush a jackrabbit from its resting or eating place along the roadside.

Early settlers in the Southwest dubbed this animal the "jackass rabbit," a name that was later shortened to "jackrabbit." Actually this creature is a hare, not a rabbit, but the inaccurate name persisted.

Hares such as the jackrabbit are lankier, leaner, and larger than rabbits such as the common cottontail, which also inhabits the desert. The hare's long, powerful legs, which give it a more muscular look, and its prominent ears, which grow to six or seven inches in length, distinguish it from the smaller rabbit. Hares do not dig burrows, as do rabbits, and are born fully covered with fur and with their eyes open.

Two species of hares inhabit the West—the white-tailed jackrabbit and the black-tailed jackrabbit (here the adjectives are more accurate). You will find the white-tail on the prairies and in the mountains of the Northwest while the black-tail inhabits the deserts of the Southwest.

The black-tailed jackrabbit is seventeen to twenty-one inches long, weighs from three to seven pounds, and has a gray brown body with white undersides. It has the appropriate black streak on its tail and black tips on its long ears.

These huge ears perform like a dish antenna, collecting any nearby sounds. They also help the jackrabbit dissipate heat from its body, much like the ears of the kit fox. If you get a look at a jackrabbit's ears with the sunlight behind them, you can see through the translucent membranes with small blood vessels running through them.

The jackrabbit relies on speed and broken field running to evade its chief enemy, the coyote, as well as the fox, bobcat, and owl. It is a master of such evasive action, running at speeds of up to thirty-five miles an hour with its ears folded back alongside its head, dodging this way and that with zigzag swerves, making leaps of up to twenty feet. Cowboys say they have seen jackrabbits jump over horses.

Like many desert animals the jackrabbit forages for food from early evening until the following dawn. On its nocturnal rambles it nibbles on cactus, mesquite, and other succulents, which provide it not only nourishment but also water. A slanted cut on the twig of a bush is a good indication that the twig was nipped by a jackrabbit; a deer leaves a pinched-off cut.

After consuming, on average, a pound of vegetation per night, the jackrabbit returns to its resting place, or "form," by daybreak. Each jack has three or four forms scattered around its large territory, generally under the cover of a bush or rock. Here, protected from the sun and partly hidden, the jack scratches out a shallow depression and sits or sleeps until the cool of the evening.

A female jackrabbit produces two or three broods annually, each containing two to five babies. To prepare for the births, she may dig a shallow nest and fill it with fur from her body, or she may simply hop under a bush and give birth. Within hours the young jacks can move about; they quickly learn to hop. Their mother nurses them for three to four weeks while they learn to eat tender plants. The rapidly growing youngsters are on their own after about a month.

Peccary (Javelina)

It looks like a pig, grunts like a pig, smells like a pig, but it is not exactly a pig—it is a peccary. In the Southwest they call it a javelina (pronounced HAV-a-leena), using the name given to it by the Spanish.

The peccary is the only native pig found in the United States. The familiar domesticated pig and the wild hog that inhabit several states did not originate in North America; both were imported from Europe and have different characteristics.

The peccary, for example, has three toes on each hindfoot, while the wild hog and domesticated pig have four; it has thirty-eight teeth instead of the hog's fortyfour. Furthermore, the peccary's upper tusks curve downward like spears. Those of a hog curve upward.

A peccary is smaller than the typical domestic pig or hog. It is about two feet tall, weighs about forty to fifty pounds, and is surprisingly light on its feet. Its coat is a mixture of black and gray hairs, giving it a grizzled look. It has a large head and long nose, which ends in a typical piglike flat pink snout. With its relatively poor eyesight, the peccary may smell or hear you before it sees you.

If you are downwind from the animal, you may smell it. The peccary exudes a substance from a gland on its back rear that has a strong musky smell. These animals

peccary

The peccary, or javelina, an animal of the desert, eats coarse plants such as cactus, as well as nuts, fruits, berries, and grubs. Its complex stomach can digest even spiny desert plants.

rub against one another to transfer the smell to all the members of a herd. They also back into a bush or tall grass, transferring their odor to the vegetation to mark their territory.

If you do see a peccary, it will most likely be running in a herd of five to fifteen animals. A herd includes both males and females, quite unlike the deer family, for example, in which does and fawns band together while males forage for themselves. A peccary herd, usually led by a dominant male, has a well-defined pecking order of leaders and followers and often stays together for life.

Look around for shallow holes dug by these animals, black droppings, or masses of rounded hoofprints, which reveal that a herd of grazing animals has passed through. You have no need to worry about safety when you encounter peccaries; they will run away. Only if cornered, wildlife observers say, would a peccary ever attack a human.

Like any pig, peccaries are not known for their neatness. One ranger observed a band of peccaries drinking at a water hole near the Saguaro National Monument's visitor center, wading through the water and muddying the water hole. After the peccaries left a coyote appeared at the water hole. It took one look at the muddy water and seemed to turn up its nose. You could imagine it cursing those clumsy desert dwellers, the peccaries, as it trotted away.

The peccary subsists on nuts, mesquite beans, berries, fruit, cactus, grubs, and bird's eggs. It even eats the spiky prickly pear cactus, especially during a drought season when the succulent provides needed moisture. Observers have seen the peccary knock a prickly pear pad or leaf to the ground, hold it down with a forefoot, and then peel back the skin to get at the soft flesh beneath. The animal can survive in the hot desert for only a week without water or succulent forage. Reports that peccaries stomp and eat rattlesnakes are probably untrue; biologists say they avoid rattlers.

Peccaries know no fixed mating season, but breed at any time. After four months the female retires to a cool place in the rocks or shrubs and bears two reddish brown piglets, occasionally more. The mother cleans and nurses her offspring and the next day leads them back to the protection of the herd. Weaned after six weeks, they remain with their mother for about a year before taking their place in the social order of the herd.

Kangaroo Rat

kangaroo rat

Several species of smaller animals of the arid desert never need to seek a water source. The kangaroo rat, pocket mouse, and their close relatives get all the moisture they need from their main food source, seeds.

These little rodents—easy to overlook and difficult to observe because they are nocturnal—are surprisingly well-adapted to this hot, dry environment.

The kangaroo rat's six-inch tail is longer than its body, which measures about five inches. It has oversized legs and feet that enable it to hop lightly across the hot desert landscape to escape its foes, leaping like a tiny, erratic kangaroo. By whipping its tail to one side, the agile animal can execute a ninety-degree turn in midair to throw off a pursuer; in a single leap the kangaroo rat can cover six feet.

Its strategy for obtaining and conserving water involves staying in its cool underground burrow during the heat of the day, then coming out at night to gather the seeds that constitute some ninety percent of its diet. The starchy seed kernels provide the kangaroo rat with water as well as food; they are metabolized by its digestive system, thereby eliminating the need for the rodent to drink. The rat also has very efficient kidneys that concentrate its wastes and further prevent the loss of body fluid.

The rat gathers and temporarily stores seeds in shallow caches it digs under the sand. Later it stuffs the seeds into its two expandable cheek pouches and carries them to a storeroom in its burrow. Using its two front feet to press in its cheeks, it empties the two pouches like saddlebags into the larder that will carry the rodent through the winter months. Favorite seeds are those of the mesquite, creosotebush, ragweed, Russian thistle, and various grasses.

Another key to its survival in the desert is the kangaroo rat's acute hearing, which is four times sharper than a human's. Its thin-walled skull and a middle ear larger than its brain enable the animal to catch the sound of an owl's beating wings or a rattlesnake's slithering movements through the sand. Such sounds trigger instant flight.

The kangaroo rat builds its burrow by kicking sand into a pile with its hindfeet. During the day it plugs up burrow entrances to keep out predators like the coyote, fox, and snake. A burrow may grow to a height of three feet and a width of fifteen feet, and it may have a dozen entrances, the main one wide enough for a fox to stick its nose in. But inside the tunnels narrow and often come to dead ends. To further discourage a marauder, the rat thumps its feet on the floor of its burrow, making a drumming sound.

If caught in the open, the kangaroo rat has another tactic. It turns its back on its enemy and uses its strong hindfeet to kick sand into the attacker's face. Despite these defensive schemes, however, desert rats and mice make up a large part of the diet of larger predators.

The kangaroo rat sticks close to its home burrow, covering perhaps a third of an acre in its nighttime foraging. It is strongly territorial and readily opposes another kangaroo rat or desert mouse that tries to sneak into its neighborhood. If two rats meet they stand upright, circling and jabbing like miniature boxers. Squealing at each other, they use their most potent weapon, their feet, to kick as they leap at each other, until one of them gains superiority.

These desert rats lead a solitary existence except during breeding season when they seek out mates. Female kangaroo rats generally have two or more litters of two to five offspring a year, but will postpone breeding entirely for a time if the land suffers an extended drought resulting in a lack of food. The young remain in their nest of grass in the burrow for more than a month, reaching adult size in six weeks. In favorable years the number of kangaroo rats in an area may increase tenfold.

Another common desert rodent is the pocket mouse, which is smaller than the kangaroo rat and does not have the rat's large rear legs and feet; instead of hopping, the mouse moves about on all fours. Other rodents found in the desert are the white-footed mouse and the woodrat. You might run across a woodrat at dusk as it embarks on its nightly search for food and material to add to its above-ground nest. Look under a bush for its nest, a pile of debris consisting mostly of sticks and cactus joints.

If you are walking a desert trail in the morning, cast your eye under the bushes and in the sand for tracks made by the nighttime meanderings of these humble but remarkable little desert animals.

Desert Tortoise

A good time to look for a desert tortoise is after a rainshower. This is when the tortoise is intent on finding a puddle of water to replenish the natural reservoir it carries beneath its high-domed shell.

Although it gets the benefit of some water from its vegetarian diet of grasses, blossoms, and succulents, the tortoise relies on an occasional drink to fill up its relatively immense bladder. Biologists calculate that a thirsty tortoise can drink enough water at such an opportunity to increase its weight by as much as forty-three percent. With its water tank thus filled, the tortoise is ready to face even an extended drought.

This slowpoke of the desert is called a tortoise because it is a turtle that lives on land; turtles that live in water have flipperlike feet and a more streamlined shell. Turtles as a group are the only reptiles that possess an outer protective shell.

The tortoise has short, heavy, clublike legs with toes on its rear feet. Its hip bones and shoulder bones, unlike those of any other animal, fold up inside its shell when the animal withdraws in the face of danger. Few other animals have such a quick or effective means of protection.

We saw this reflex in action one day as we drove a desert park road. A tortoise, a foot long and dusty gray in color, trudged along the roadside. As soon as we alighted to get a better look, it retracted its landing gear and lay still. If you hadn't seen it move, you would have thought it was a gray rock.

The tortoise, like all reptiles, is cold-blooded and cannot control its body temperature, which varies with the temperature of its surroundings. As a consequence, reptiles are most active in late morning after sunning themselves to bring their bodies up to "operating temperature." As the day grows hot they seek out a shady spot so as not to heat up too much. In the afternoon they may wander about again, returning to their burrow in the cool of the evening.

In winter the tortoise hibernates in the burrow it digs with its shovellike front legs. The burrow is approximately as wide as the tortoise is long, thus allowing the animal to turn around in its underground home. The average depth of a burrow is about ten feet.

This slow-moving desert animal is found in the dry regions of California, Nevada, Utah, and Arizona. A tortoise normally forages a home range of ten to one hun-

desert tortoise

The desert tortoise has two main means of defense: blending into its surroundings and withdrawing into its shell. Few animals possess such quick and effective ways of protecting themselves.

dred acres, often living its entire life within a mile of where it was hatched.

In spring it feeds on the juicy green annual plants that grow after winter rains, sometimes consuming three or four percent of its weight to rehydrate itself after hibernation.

In early May, desert vegetation begins to dry out, but the tortoise continues to feed. It can tolerate both mild dehydration and a build-up of salts within its body until its reservoir of water can be replenished. This capacity helps the tortoise get through the late spring and early summer drought.

By June it reduces its food intake and spends an increasing amount of time in its burrow. By remaining underground the tortoise reduces its water loss from both evaporation and respiration.

A tortoise does not breed until it is about fifteen years old. Breeding activity commences in spring after the animal emerges from its four- to five-month hibernation. A male vying for a female's attention often engages in a jousting match with another male, using a horn on its underside to ram and push its opponent, sometimes overturning the other tortoise. This can be fatal; if the overturned tortoise cannot right itself, it will die in the desert heat.

A female tortoise digs a hole, four inches deep, at or inside the entrance to her burrow. She lays a clutch of eggs in the cavity, then covers them with dirt that she scoops into the hole with her hindfeet. Finally, she urinates on the spot, probably to mask the site from predators.

After three months the eggs hatch and the 1½-inch baby turtles dig their way through the overlying sand to the surface. A newborn, covered with a leathery shell (rather than a hard one) and unprotected by either of its parents, faces many perils. The baby tortoise can easily become prey for a kit fox, coyote, Gila monster, or snake. But those that survive probably live a long life once their protective shell hardens. Desert tortoises kept in captivity have lived for as long as seventy years.

Lizards

One of the most common animals of the desert—but not necessarily the easiest to see—is the lizard.

Scurrying across the desert floor, it twists this way and that, swishes its tail, darts under a bush or into a rock crevice, or digs itself rapidly into the sand, quickly disappearing from sight.

Lizards are reptiles that are closely related to the snake. As you become more acquainted with desert life you will find that lizards come in all sizes, shapes, and colors—from the beige lizards a few inches long of the southwestern United States to the huge Komodo monitor of Indonesia, which grows to ten feet in length and weighs as much as three hundred pounds. Worldwide, biologists have identified an amazing three thousand different species of lizards.

You need only look around you on the ground as you walk the trails to see these agile denizens of the desert. Lizards of this region have dry, scaly skin and clawed toes that enable them to dig in loose sand. Almost all are harmless.

They reproduce, as do tortoises and snakes, by laying eggs. The female usually lays her eggs in or near her burrow and covers them with sand. Incubated by the warm sun, the eggs hatch and tiny lizards emerge. Defenseless, they are immediately on their own with no parental help.

A good time to look for lizards is in the morning on a sunny day. Like tortoises and snakes, lizards are cold-blooded. A lizard often crawls out of its burrow, where it has spent the night, and stretches out on a rock in the sand to bask in the sunlight and warm up. Once warmed, it is ready to begin its daily food hunt. When the ground

lizard

becomes too hot at midday, the lizard moves into a shady spot or burrows into cooler sand beneath the surface.

While hunting for its next meal, a lizard takes maximum advantage of its high degree of protective coloration. The three-inch-long zebra-tailed lizard, for example, sits motionless, its mottled brown body and black-striped tail blending into the granular desert surface, and raises itself on its forelegs to get a good look around. When an unsuspecting beetle, termite, or grasshopper comes along, it scurries over and snaps it up.

Protective coloration is also vital to the horned lizard. This bizarre-looking animal cannot run as fast as most desert lizards. Instead it adapts its color to its surroundings: it is blackish in a lava flow area, reddish on red soil, and orange in the Painted Desert of Arizona. It

"Please Do Not Feed the Wildlife"

Pulling into a picnic area at Lake Irene in Rocky Mountain National Park, we saw a doe mule deer grazing in the grass. We watched a woman walk over to the animal, hold out her hand and offer it popcorn.

"It's real tame," she said to us over her shoulder. "Look, it won't run from you or anything!"

Marge and I stepped to one side and watched. In the next fifteen minutes no fewer than thirty picnickers either fed or were photographed with this "tame" deer. The handouts included crackers, candy, and potato chips as well as popcorn.

Every visitor to a national park or wildlife refuge has heard the ranger warnings and read the signs: "Do Not Feed the Wildlife." Even so, people have a strong tendency to offer food and thereby control an animal's behavior. Rangers must continually remind visitors and explain the numerous reasons for their warnings. Among the problems they cite are these:

Bad nutrition.   Giving "people food" to deer, rangers tell you, not only results in poor nutrition but can actually harm the animal's digestive system. That goes for seemingly nutritious food, such as carrots and apples, as well. A deer's remarkable four-chambered stomach is made to digest cellulose. Bacteria in the stomach gradually digest the woody material as it passes from chamber to chamber. "People food" upsets the deer's digestion, introducing "empty calories" and clogging the deer's arteries. Rangers at Glacier National Park told us that people food also can cause a ground squirrel to store up "white fat" instead of the more wholesome "brown fat" that provides sustenance for the squirrel during its long winter hibernation. In effect, park visitors who feed wildlife make it more difficult for them to develop the nutritional balance they need to survive winter. Feeding the animals literally kills them with kindness. It was painful for us to realize that the "tame" deer being fed by park visitors might later be unable to survive the harsh Rocky Mountain winter.

Dependence upon handouts.   An animal that becomes dependent on handouts of people food can become so accustomed to the artificial food supply that it becomes unable to forage for itself. At Yellowstone, a ranger explained that some coyotes have become so dependent on handouts that they have lost their skill at

has an additional defense: the spiky horns protruding from the back of its head and along its spine make it an unappetizing meal for a predator such as a snake.

A different defense strategy is employed by the chuckwalla, a large lizard with a body up to eight inches long and a fat tail. When threatened, this harmless lizard squeezes into a rocky crevice, gulping air to inflate its body, effectively wedging itself between the rocks. Thus situated, chuckwallas are almost impossible to remove.

The largest lizard found within the boundaries of the United States and one of only two poisonous lizards in the world is the Gila (pronounced HEE-la) monster. It is easily recognizable by its bright orange and black coloration. Its bulbous body is about a foot long and its fat tail adds another six inches, leading you to the accurate

---

hunting. As a predator, the coyote must hunt prey to survive. In winter, when visitors leave and the handouts cease, the coyote might starve. At Great Smoky Mountain National Park a black bear was found dead; the cause of death—an aluminum can in its stomach.

Concentration of wildlife.   Providing an artificial food supply is likely to attract a number of animals to one location, drawing them away from their normal feeding territories and increasing their risk of spreading diseases among one another. Additionally, animals attracted by food to roadsides are more apt to be killed by cars.

Disruption of animal social life.   Although people tend to think of wild animals as living unstructured lives, most animals are part of rather rigid social systems. These systems tend to regulate population size and give each animal a social framework in which to live. When people interfere with that structure by drawing animals to one location to feed, the general stress level increases dramatically. Reproduction drops and the animals become more susceptible to diseases.

Harm to people.   Not only the well-being of animals but the well-being of visitors themselves may be affected by thoughtless feeding of wildlife. Feeding and petting a deer, for example, can allow a tiny tick that sometimes clings to a deer's hide to attach itself to the skin of a person. The tick, scarcely the size of a poppy seed, can cause Lyme disease, the most prevalent tick-borne disease in the country, one that infects several thousand people each year. If not promptly diagnosed and treated with antibiotics, Lyme disease produces a rash and flulike symptoms, which may include fever, nausea, soreness, headaches, neck strain, backaches, and profound fatigue. In addition, raccoons, skunks, and other animals that scavenge in campgrounds can transmit rabies.

Even a wildlife enthusiast's physical safety can be in jeopardy. Rangers at Shenandoah National Park tell of one woman who tried to get a large white-tailed buck to stick its head, antlers and all, into her car window so that she could feed it. Fortunately, the buck's head was unable to fit. Otherwise, they say, the strong animal could have panicked and ripped into both the passenger and the car. On another occasion a boy placed an apple in his mouth and encouraged a deer to take it directly out of his mouth—at serious risk to the young visitor.

So when you see the sign "Do Not Feed the Wildlife," take it seriously. As one ranger said, "A national park is a wild place. Let's keep it that way—and the animals too."

conclusion that it is slow-moving. Its favorite foods are bird and tortoise eggs.

If forced to defend itself, the Gila monster will bite its enemy, transmitting venom through its teeth to immobilize an aggressor such as a coyote, kit fox, or owl. A human, if bitten by a Gila monster, may suffer swelling of the bitten area and possibly chills and nausea, but there is no record of this lizard's bite proving fatal.

Most lizards hibernate from fall until spring, burrowing beneath the ground where the temperature remains fairly constant through the chill of winter. The desert iguana, for example, a large lizard with a grayish body and a long tail, burrows about four inches beneath the surface. Here it lies, deep enough to protect itself from the surface chill but shallow enough so that it can feel the first warmth of sun in the spring.

To prepare for this long dormant spell, the iguana feeds avidly on the flowers, fruits, and leaves of desert plants such as the creosotebush, encelia, verbena, coldenia, indigo bush, and burro bush. It also snaps up blister beetles and ants to help it store the fat it needs to survive its long winter sleep. Although threatening in appearance, the iguana presents no hazard to people.

Snakes

As you walk desert trails in the daytime you will be unlikely to observe any of the several species of snakes that live here. Most desert snakes hunt at night when their favorite prey—rodents, lizards, and other snakes—are also out and about.

The one exception is the whipsnake, which needs daylight to see its prey. The color of this long, slender snake varies from pale orange to black, reflecting the predominant color of its surroundings. You can identify it by the horizontal stripes that run along its body. The whipsnake, although nonpoisonous, may grow to a formidable seven feet in length.

snake

Most snakes have poor eyesight, but the whipsnake forages by sight, lifting its head several inches off the ground to peer around. It moves its head from side to side (probably to increase its depth perception to better gauge the distance to its quarry), then strikes and seizes its prey. It also can climb a tree to search birds' nests for eggs. The whipsnake is the fastest-moving snake in the United States; biologists have measured it crawling at about three miles an hour.

Other desert-dwelling snakes forage after nightfall. They follow the familiar pattern of many animals of the desert, seeking out a shady spot to escape the daytime heat, then traveling within their territory between dusk and dawn as temperatures become cooler. Exposure to the direct rays of the midday sun has been known to kill a sidewinder rattlesnake in ten minutes.

A snake's sensory perception is adapted to its night-time hunting. It uses its tongue instead of its eyes to explore the surrounding environment. As a snake's tongue flicks in and out of its mouth, it carries traces of odors from the air or anything it touches into a pair of sense organs in the roof of its mouth, an area with a sensitivity to odors that augments the snake's nostrils.

Poisonous snakes, called pit vipers, have another sophisticated detection device as well. Two small pits that lie between the nostrils and the eyes hold delicate heat-detecting membranes that sense the close presence of warm-blooded prey such as a rat or a mouse.

Although you may not see a snake, you might see evidence of its presence—a snake skin. The scaly skin of a snake, unlike that of a mammal or a bird, does not stretch as the animal grows. As a result, the snake sheds its skin from time to time, leaving it with a new skin slightly larger than the old one. To rid itself of the old skin, a snake rubs against the branch of a bush or a rock; the skin is like parchment, and peels off like a glove pulled off wrong side out.

A snake moves about by contracting its body muscles, producing a horizontal wave from head to tail. The scales on its underside grip the surface and the snake propels itself forward. A sidewinder rattlesnake uses a different method. Using its head and tail for support, it loops its body sideways, then retracts its head and tail. Look for a sidewinder's track, a series of parallel lines in soft sand.

The rattlesnake, a pit viper that inhabits the Southwestern desert, is a venomous snake—probably the most dangerous in the United States. There are ten species of rattlesnakes, ranging in size from the small, eighteen-inch sidewinder to the large Western diamondback, which has been known to reach seven feet in length.

The rattler attacks its prey by coiling itself into an S-shape to get the necessary leverage to launch the front half of its body and seize its prey. Its venom paralyzes and kills its victim. Rattlesnakes stalk pocket mice, kangaroo rats, woodrats, and ground squirrels, as well as smaller snakes.

A snake can swallow a creature several times the diameter of its body. The jaws of all snakes are held together with ligaments that stretch during feeding so that the mouth distends to several times its normal size. The snake's jaws move forward one side at a time as the reptile's needlelike teeth draw the victim inward until it disappears. Enzymes in the snake's digestive system enable it to digest everything except hair or feathers in seventy-two hours. A snake drinks by partly submerging its head, expanding its lower jaw and sucking water into its throat.

Most female snakes reproduce by laying a clutch of up to twelve eggs in a secluded place, then crawling away and leaving the eggs to hatch unattended about 1½ months later. A female rattler, on the other hand, gives birth to live offspring. The eggs develop within the mother's body until some two to twenty-five rattlers are born.

A baby rattlesnake is born with but one rattle on its tail; it will add a new one each time it sheds its skin. But you cannot simply count the rattles on a rattler to determine its age; the string of rattles usually breaks off after the rattles number about twelve. Then the snake begins to grow a new set.

Rattlesnakes and other species hibernate during winter months. Finding a haven such as an unused rodent hole, they crawl in, curl up, and fall into a trancelike sleep that lasts until spring.

Other snakes of the desert Southwest are the poisonous Western coral snake and the nonpoisonous king snake and gopher snake.

Rangers say that snakes often hole up in a brush pile, fallen log, or rock crevice. Consequently, they suggest wearing high-top boots and advise against sticking your hand or foot into any hole or opening whose interior you cannot see.

Snakes and other creatures of the desert prove that, despite the oppressive heat and lack of water, dry regions offer a varied collection of animals that have successfully adapted to the desert's rigorous conditions.

CHAPTER 10

Your World Opens Up

A century ago, cowboys who drove herds of cattle across the plains would sit around the evening campfire spinning yarns, some about fanciful animals. One cowhand imagined for his sidekicks an animal called a "jackelope," a creature with the body of a jackrabbit and the antlers of a pronghorn. The male of the species, he related—with a twinkle in his eye—had wings!

Like many a cowboy's tall tale, this one caught on; the "jackelope" has been embedded in western folklore ever since. The mythical animal is sometimes described in all its glory as a playful joke to test the credulity of an outsider not familiar with western wildlife.

But not even the mythical "jackelope" possesses the startling characteristics of some of the animals we saw and learned about during our trips through the sanctuaries that protect the nation's wildlife. From rangers and biologists we gained new insights into the diversity of animal life being protected for present and future Americans.

These preserves—national wildlife refuges, national parks, national forests, lands administered by the Bureau of Land Management, Indian reservations, military bases, public utilities, corporate lands, and other federal, state, and county preserves—play a vital role in conserving the habitat needed to support the existing species of wild animals in this country.

At Shenandoah National Park in the Blue Ridge Mountains, for example, fifty years of conservation efforts have brought a dramatic increase in the wildlife population.

When Indians inhabited these hills, black bear and white-tailed deer were plentiful. So were elk, wolves, and even bison. Place names within the park commemorate some of these vanished species—"Elkwallow Gap" and "Wolf Run."

Then settlers moved into hollows and up on ridges, cultivating patches of land for vegetables and fruit, cutting trees for lumber and for their tanneries. Fires burned over much of the mountainous countryside. Overtrapping eliminated the beaver and hunting reduced the number of bear and deer. By the time Shenandoah was established in 1938, biologists estimated that only about ten bears were left and only a few deer.

Policies of the newly established park reversed this trend: no lumbering, no grazing of domestic livestock, no hunting, no trapping. By 1951 the number of black bears had increased to thirty; by 1988, a study concluded, no less than five hundred to six hundred bears lived in the park, which measures only one hundred miles long. White-tailed deer staged a similar strong comeback, reaching an estimated total of six thousand by 1988.

Today Shenandoah takes its place among the national sanctuaries that provide a haven for wildlife. These preserves offer a sample of wild America, a place where people can go to see untrammeled nature, a place where natural ecosystems are left undisturbed. They serve as a genetic storehouse for animal and plant species that otherwise might have disappeared; here scientists can study wild animals in their natural setting.

Visitors to national parks sometimes have trouble realizing that natural processes govern in a wilderness area, that man interferes as little as possible with nature.

One day a man rushed breathlessly up to a ranger at Yellowstone National Park, waving his arms frantically. "Do something," he shouted. "There's a grizzly bear up the trail and he's trying to kill an elk!"

The ranger quieted the man, explaining that the grizzly was a predator, that it needed to eat meat to survive and that the elk was one of the animals it preyed upon. For that reason, he said, unless a visitor's safety was threatened, the park staff would do nothing to stop the actions of the grizzly. As the ranger told his colleagues later, he felt that after twenty minutes of explanation the visitor had accepted the need for predators in the animal world—intellectually, that is, but perhaps not emotionally.

Planning to Observe Wildlife

To get the most out of a trip that includes seeing wild animals at national wildlife refuges, national parks, or national forests—or on a field trip to a state or local park—it might be a good idea to spend some time making plans. Doing so will help you choose the most suitable time of year and thus improve your chances of seeing wild animals. For example, you won't see bears,

woodchucks, or marmots in midwinter when these animals hibernate and are out of sight; on the other hand,
winter viewing of elk or bison could turn into an exciting
adventure.

An excellent time to visit Yellowstone National Park,
rangers say, is in spring or fall. From May through June
bison, elk, and pronghorn are concentrated in the low
valleys. It is calving time among the herds; by summer
most of the hoofed browsers and grazers move into the
less accessible high country. Fall is the breeding season
for elk, moose, mule deer, bison, and pronghorn. At this
time of year family groups or entire herds congregate,
making it an exciting time to witness the social interaction of animals.

Chapters 5 through 9 describe the animals found in
different sections of the country. Other sources are available to tell you which preserves are best for viewing
these wild animals.

The National Geographic Society (17th and M
Streets, Washington, DC 20036) publishes two references
that help. A wall map entitled "America's Federal Lands"
displays all of the nation's national parks, national wildlife refuges, national forests and grasslands, Bureau of
Land Management public lands, Indian lands, military
properties, and other public lands. A companion booklet, "A Guide to Our Federal Lands," gives brief descriptions of the wildlife, other resources, and activities found
at each of these public landholdings, which encompass
more than 700 million acres—nearly one-third of the
nation.

To help you choose the national parks along your
route that offer the most promising opportunities to
watch wildlife, you might refer to *The Complete Guide
to America's National Parks*, published by the National
Park Foundation and distributed by Viking Press, New
York, NY 10010.

For a detailed description of the wildlife you can
expect to see at the 448 national wildlife refuges in the
nation, you can refer to *Guide to the National Wildlife
Refuges*, by Laura and William Riley (Doubleday, New
York, NY 10103, 1979). The authors devote a page or
more to the wildlife at each refuge and how best to
observe the animals.

For information on national forests, *Field Guide to
U.S. National Forests*, by Robert Mohlenbrock (Congdon
and Weed Inc., 298 Fifth Avenue, New York, NY 10001)
will be useful.

Several states assist wildlife watchers. Oregon has
erected more than one hundred state highway signs im-
printed with a logotype of a pair of binoculars and the
words "Wildlife Viewing Area." An eighty-page booklet,
"Wildlife Viewing Guide," lists locations that animals frequent and describes the sites. Copies are available from
Defenders of Wildlife, 333 South State Street, Suite 173,
Lake Oswego, OR 97034.

Tennessee has erected signs along its highways designating promising "Wildlife Observation Areas" and offering the use of side trails, blinds, and observation towers to wildlife enthusiasts.

In Wyoming a visitor center at Cheyenne acquaints travelers with the best places to see wildlife in the state. West Virginia each summer holds a "nongame wildlife weekend" at a state park, offering discussions and field trips to discover animals and plants of the forest and field.

Do not overlook state, county, and city parks, many of which support wildlife populations. An outstanding example, mentioned earlier, is Custer State Park in South Dakota, which manages a large bison herd as well as bighorn sheep, mountain goats, elk, deer, and pronghorns.

A number of states allow citizens to designate a small amount of their state income tax to preserve endangered species and to build wildlife-watching facilities such as towers, boardwalks, and nature trails.

Getting Acquainted with Wildlife

The more you know about the animals you expect to view, the rangers emphasize, the more readily you will be able to spot them.

"A few hours spent getting to know the appearance and habits of the animals you hope to see will make for a much more productive observation experience," said Clyde Lockwood, a former chief naturalist at Glacier National Park.

In preparing to observe wildlife, concentrate on the basic characteristics and habits of the animals, including their size and color. Knowing that the pronghorn of the prairie is cinnamon with distinctive white markings on its neck, underbelly, and rump will help you distinguish it from the brownish gray mule deer with no markings on its neck or underbelly, even though the two animals are about the same size.

Learn the habitat an animal prefers, the food it likes to eat, the seasonal activities it will be involved in, and whether it leads a solitary life or travels in a group.

You will likely find a moose around water, for example, since much of its diet is aquatic plants. Beaver, of course, live in water; they make it easy for you to locate them by cutting down whole groves of trees and by building an unmistakable lodge in the pond they have dammed up.

A little time spent reading about animals will teach you the difference between, for example, a marmot and a pika. Both animals scurry around the high mountains. Both, you will discover, make a whistling sound: the

A bull elk stands guard over one of Yellowstone National Park's several elk herds. Elk usually leave the forest's protective cover in late afternoon or evening to graze in an open meadow.

chirp of the marmot and the intermittent squeak of the pika. But learning that the marmot is yellowish brown, has a bushy tail, and is about the size of a small cat, will keep you from confusing it with the gray brown pika, which has no tail and is about the size and shape of a guinea pig.

Yet another source of information is the *Field Guide to the Mammals of North America North of Mexico*, by William Henry Burt, one of the well-known Peterson field guide series (Houghton Mifflin Company, Boston, MA 02108).

To get a firsthand look at some of these animals before you see them in the wild, you might pay a visit to your local zoo (see pages 7–8).

Ranger Assistance

Other information sources await you at each refuge or park visitor center. As you approach a number of national parks you may tune your car radio to a traveler's information service, a prerecorded announcement detailing park visitor hours, its major resources, and any special events scheduled for the next few days.

Upon your arrival, it is a good idea to head for the visitor center, where films, slide shows, displays, and exhibits will further orient you to the park. At Yellowstone and Great Smoky Mountains national parks, for example, we found helpful wildlife exhibits that included mounted specimens that give an up-close look at some of the animals you might view in the wild.

You will be able to pick up folders on wildlife and maps of hiking trails that should help you plan. In many parks, a well-stocked book store offers additional books, booklets, field guides, and tape and video cassettes.

Best of all, you will have the opportunity to consult with the ranger or volunteer behind the counter, who can answer many of your questions, inform you of the latest animal sightings reported by the ranger patrols, provide you with the weather forecast, and pass along tips to make your wildlife watching more productive.

Rangers can tell you which trails lead through promising animal habitat, where water sources and natural salt licks attract wildlife, and where grazing lands and berry patches provide good feeding areas. They also will give you the schedule of ranger talks and ranger-led

At Chincoteague National Wildlife Refuge visitors discover that each wild pony has recognizable individual markings. Rangers and interpreters at refuges, parks, and forests point out such interesting facts to help people observe the nation's wildlife.

walks, excellent opportunities to go into the field with the guidance of the ranger's firsthand knowledge. Without them, Marge and I would never have learned that bighorn sheep are so attracted to any sweet or salty substance that they will sometimes wander into a parking area to lick up spilled radiator coolant or lick an automobile's tires.

Rangers also are prepared with safety tips for visitors. At Wind Cave National Park a ranger warned visitors to give the right-of-way to any bison herd crossing a park road. As a park visitor, he explained, you are an intruder in the bison's domain. "Observe, but don't interfere," he advised. "Otherwise you may come away with a dented fender."

If you are interested in the park's wildlife management program, the ranger on duty can probably fill you in on wildlife research projects currently under way. At Great Smoky Mountains National Park we learned how park biologists had attached small radio transmitters to river otters they had reintroduced, then tracked the otters by radio to study their habits, define their range, and see how many survived. At Yellowstone and Grand Teton national parks, biologists are studying the feasibility of reintroducing the gray wolf, a predator that would reestablish the balance of nature in these ecosystems.

Now you are ready to take the tour road or hike the trails. Remember that rangers in many parks and refuges advise you to take the tour road to get an overview of the wildlife from your car, van, or recreational vehicle.

Staying in your car gives you several advantages. It permits you to cover more territory than you could on foot. As mentioned previously, it serves as an effective blind, shielding you from the animals. Your car also disguises your human scent, which is quickly sensed by animals. Park animals are usually accustomed to automobiles on a tour road. But as soon as you get out of your car, they pick up your scent and movement. If they sense a threat, they may move quickly away.

In addition to viewing animals along the tour road, you may want to take a hike or go backpacking along park trails identified by the rangers as paths that lead through promising wildlife habitat. Here you might make use of some of the wildlife-watching techniques outlined in Chapter 4 to look for clues, signs, and sounds of the animals around you. Rangers emphasize repeatedly that early morning and late afternoon and evening are the times when animals are most visible. Remember that you are a visitor in the animals' domain; walk softly and converse quietly, blending as much as possible into the background.

Listen for animal sounds around you. The importance of listening closely as you search for wildlife was emphasized for us the day we talked with Superintendent Richard Marks at Grand Canyon National Park. "Folks need to learn not only to look for animals but to listen for them," he told us as we stood looking out at the magnificent Grand Canyon. "The sound of a hawk is different from the sound of an owl. A coyote's howl is a lot different from a fox's bark. You may never see a particular animal you're looking for, but if you're listening for its call you can still experience it."

Shortly after talking with Dick Marks, Marge and I took a hike along a foot trail that winds along the edge of the South Rim of the canyon. The late afternoon sun shone beneath the clouds that sailed overhead, casting long shadows into the canyon.

As we followed the trail around a rocky point, a young couple excitedly pointed to a spot on the canyon wall. There, two bighorn sheep calmly foraged on the narrow ledge of a cliff that dropped several hundred feet into the canyon. The bighorns, sure-footed as ever, picked their way along the ledge, nibbling the sparse vegetation. As the ledge narrowed to a dead end, one of the bighorns rose up on its hind legs, pivoted, then dropped back down, nimbly reversing direction—all this while seemingly oblivious to the four humans who watched in wonderment.

A scene like this, we reflected, epitomizes the lure of wildlife watching. Here is the moment you hope and plan for, the magic moment when you peer into a wild animal's world without intruding into its environment. We could enjoy the privilege of watching as the two sheep, challenged to find food in their harsh habitat, passed one of nature's sternest tests.

For a wildlife watcher it is a high privilege to observe a wild animal, unfettered by constraints, fulfilling its natural role within its environment. It is the observer's reward for being in the right place at the right time.

Where to Write for Information

State Park Departments

Division of Parks
Alabama Department of Conservation &
  Natural Resources
64 N. Union Street
Montgomery, Alabama 36130

Parks and Outdoor Recreation
Alaska Department of Natural Resources
400 Willoughby
Juneau, Alaska 99801

Arkansas Department of Parks and
  Tourism
One Capitol Mall
Little Rock, Arkansas 72201

California Department of Parks and
  Recreation
1416 Ninth Street
P.O. Box 942896
Sacramento, California 94296-0001

Parks and Outdoor Recreation
Colorado Department of Natural
  Resources
1313 Sherman Street, Room 618
Denver, Colorado 80203

Office of State Parks & Recreation
Connecticut Department of
  Environmental Protection
State Office Building
165 Capitol Avenue
Hartford, Connecticut 06106

Parks and Recreation
Delaware Department of Natural
  Resources
89 Kings Highway
P.O. Box 1401
Dover, Delaware 19903

Recreation and Parks
Florida Department of Natural Resources
Marjory Stoneman Douglas Building
Tallahassee, Florida 32303

Parks and Recreation Historic Sites
Georgia Department of Natural Resources
Floyd Towers East
205 Butler Street
Atlanta, Georgia 30334

Parks and Recreation
Hawaii Department of Land and Natural
  Resources
Box 621
Honolulu, Hawaii 96809

Idaho Department of Parks and
  Recreation
Statehouse
Boise, Idaho 83720

Wildlife Resources Division
Illinois Department of Conservation
Lincoln Tower Plaza
524 S. Second Street
Springfield, Illinois 62706

Division of State Parks
Indiana Department of Natural Resources
608 State Office Building
Indianapolis, Indiana 46204

Parks, Recreation, and Preserves Division
Iowa Department of Natural Resources
Wallace Building
E. 9th and Grand Avenues
Des Moines, Iowa 50319-0034

Kansas Department of Wildlife and Parks
900 Jackson Street, Suite 502
Topeka, Kansas 66612-1220

Kentucky Department of Parks
Capital Plaza Building, 10th Floor
Frankfort, Kentucky 40601

Louisiana Office of State Parks
P.O. Drawer 1111
Baton Rouge, Louisiana 70821

Parks and Recreation
Maine Department of Conservation
State House, Station #22
Augusta, Maine 04333

Forest, Parks, and Wildlife Services
Maryland Department of Natural
  Resources
Tawes State Office Building
Annapolis, Maryland 21401

Forests and Parks
Massachusetts Department of
  Environmental Management
100 Cambridge Street
Boston, Massachusetts 02202

Parks Division
Michigan Department of Natural
  Resources
Box 30028
Lansing, Michigan 48909

Parks and Recreation
Minnesota Department of Natural
  Resources
500 Lafayette Road
St. Paul, Minnesota 55155

Bureau of Recreation and Parks
Mississippi Department of Natural
  Resources
P.O. Box 10600
Jackson, Mississippi 39209

Parks, Recreation, and Historic
  Preservation
Missouri Department of Natural
  Resources
P.O. Box 176
Jefferson City, Missouri 65102

Montana Department of Fish, Wildlife,
  and Parks
1420 East Sixth
Helena, Montana 59620

Nebraska Game and Parks Commission
2200 N. 33rd Street
P.O. Box 30370
Lincoln, Nebraska 68503

Division of State Parks
Nevada Department of Conservation and
  Natural Resources
Capitol Complex, Nye Building
201 S. Fall Street
Carson City, Nevada 89710

Division of Parks
New Hampshire Department of Resources
  and Economic Development
P.O. Box 856
105 Loudon Road
Concord, New Hampshire 03301

Parks and Forestry
New Jersey Department of Environmental
  Protection
CN 404
Trenton, New Jersey 08625

Park and Recreation Division
New Mexico Natural Resources
  Department
Villagra Building
Santa Fe, New Mexico 87503

New York Office of Parks, Recreation, and
Historic Preservation
Empire State Plaza
Albany, New York 12238

Parks and Recreation
North Carolina Department of Natural
Resources and Community
Development
P. O. Box 27687
Raleigh, North Carolina 27611

North Dakota Parks and Recreation
Department
1424 W. Century Avenue, Suite 202
Bismarck, North Dakota 58501

Division of Parks and Recreation
Ohio Department of Natural Resources
65 S. Front Street
Columbus, Ohio 43215

Division of State Parks
Oklahoma Tourism and Recreation
Department
500 Will Rogers Memorial Building
Oklahoma City, Oklahoma 73105

Oregon Department of Fish and Wildlife
107 20th Street
LaGrande, Oregon 97850

Bureau of State Parks
Pennsylvania Department of
Environmental Resources
Press Office, 9th Floor, Fulton Building
Box 2063
Harrisburg, Pennsylvania 17120

Division of Parks and Recreation
Rhode Island Department of
Environmental Management
22 Hayes Street
Providence, Rhode Island 02908

South Carolina Department of Parks,
Recreation, & Tourism
Edgar A. Brown Building
1205 Pendleton Street
Columbia, South Carolina 29201

Wildlife Division
South Dakota Department of Game, Fish,
and Parks
Joe Foss Office Building
Pierre, South Dakota 57501

Division of Parks and Recreation
Tennessee Department of Conservation
701 Broadway, Customs House
Nashville, Tennessee 37203

Texas Parks and Wildlife Department
4200 Smith School Road
Austin, Texas 78744

Division of Parks and Recreation
Utah Department of Natural Resources
1636 W. North Temple
Salt Lake City, Utah 84116-3156

Vermont Department of Forests, Parks,
and Recreation
Waterbury Complex, 10 South
Waterbury, Vermont 05677

Division of Parks and Recreation
Virginia Department of Conservation and
Historic Resources
1201 Washington Building
Capitol Square
Richmond, Virginia 23219

Washington State Parks and Recreation
Commission
7150 Cleanwater Lane
Olympia, Washington 98504

Parks and Recreation
West Virginia Department of Natural
Resources
1800 Washington Street East
Charleston, West Virginia 25305

Bureau of Parks and Recreation
Wisconsin Department of Natural
Resources
Box 7921
Madison, Wisconsin 53707

Wyoming Recreation Commission
122 West 25th Street
Herschier Building
Cheyenne, Wyoming 82002

State Game Commissions

Alabama Division of Game and Fish
64 N. Union Street
Montgomery, Alabama 36104

Alaska Department of Fish and Game
P.O. Box 3-2000
Juneau, Alaska 99802

Arizona Game and Fish Department
2222 N. Greenway Road
Phoenix, Arizona 85023

Arkansas Game and Fish Commission
2 Natural Resources Drive
Little Rock, Arkansas 72205

California Department of Fish and Game
1416 9th Street
Sacramento, California 95814

Colorado Division of Wildlife
6060 Broadway
Denver, Colorado 80216

Connecticut Department of
  Environmental Protection
State Office Building
165 Capitol Avenue
Hartford, Connecticut 06115

Delaware Division of Fish and Wildlife
P.O. Box 1401
Dover, Delaware 19901

Florida Game and Freshwater Fish
  Commission
Farris Bryant Building
620 S. Meridian
Tallahassee, Florida 32301

Georgia State Game and Fish Division
205 Butler Street SE
Atlanta, Georgia 30334

Hawaii Division of Forestry & Wildlife
1151 Punchbowl Street
Honolulu, Hawaii 96813

Idaho Fish & Game Department
600 S. Walnut, Box 25
Boise, Idaho 83707

Illinois Department of Conservation
Lincoln Tower Plaza
524 S. Second Street
Springfield, Illinois 62706

Indiana Division of Fish and Wildlife
608 State Office Building
Indianapolis, Indiana 46204

Iowa Department of Natural Resources
Wallace State Office Building
East 9th and Grand Avenues
Des Moines, Iowa 50319

Kansas Fish and Game Commission
Box 54-A, R.R. #2
Pratt, Kansas 67124

Kentucky Department of Fish and
  Wildlife Resources
1 Game Farm Road
Frankfort, Kentucky 40601

Louisiana Department of Wildlife and
  Fisheries
P.O. Box 15570
Baton Rouge, Louisiana 70895

Maine Department of Inland Fisheries
  and Wildlife
284 State Street
Augusta, Maine 04333

Maryland Department of Natural
  Resources
Tawes State Office Building
Annapolis, Maryland 21401

Massachusetts Department of Fisheries,
  Wildlife and Environmental Law
  Enforcement
100 Cambridge Street
Boston, Massachusetts 02202

Michigan Department of Natural
  Resources
Stevens T. Mason Building, Box 30028
Lansing, Michigan 48909

Minnesota Department of Natural
  Resources
500 Lafayette Road
St. Paul, Minnesota 55155-4020

Mississippi Department of Wildlife
  Conservation
P.O. Box 451
Jackson, Mississippi 39205

Missouri Department of Conservation
2901 N. Ten Mile Drive
Jefferson City, Missouri 65102

Montana Department of Fish, Wildlife,
 and Parks
1420 E. 6th Avenue
Helena, Montana 59620

Nebraska Game and Park Commission
P.O. Box 30370
2200 N. 33rd
Lincoln, Nebraska 68503

Nevada Department of Wildlife
Box 10678
Reno, Nevada 89520

New Hampshire Fish and Game
 Department
34 Bridge Street
Concord, New Hampshire 03301

New Jersey Division of Fish, Game, and
 Wildlife
CN 400
Trenton, New Jersey 08625

New Mexico Game and Fish Division
New Mexico Natural Resources
 Department
Villagra Building
Santa Fe, New Mexico 87503

New York Division of Fish and Wildlife
50 Wolf Road
Albany, New York 12233

North Carolina Wildlife Resources
 Commission
Archdale Building
512 N. Salisbury Street
Raleigh, North Carolina 27611

North Dakota State Game and Fish
 Department
100 North Bismarck Expressway
Bismarck, North Dakota 58501

Ohio Division of Wildlife
Fountain Square
Columbus, Ohio 43224

Oklahoma Department of Wildlife
 Conservation
1801 N. Lincoln
P.O. Box 53465
Oklahoma City, Oklahoma 73152

Oregon Department of Fish and Wildlife
Box 59
Portland, Oregon 97207

Pennsylvania Game Commission
P.O. Box 1567
Harrisburg, Pennsylvania 17105

Rhode Island Department of
 Environmental Management
Division of Fish and Wildlife
Washington County Government Center
Wakefield, Rhode Island 02879

South Carolina Wildlife and Marine
 Resources Department
Rembert C. Dennis Building, Box 167
Columbia, South Carolina 29202

South Dakota Department of Game, Fish,
 and Parks
Sigurd Anderson Building
445 E. Capitol
Pierre, South Dakota 57501

Tennessee Wildlife Resources Agency
Box 40747
Ellington Agricultural Center
Nashville, Tennessee 37204

Texas Parks and Wildlife Department
4200 Smith School Road
Austin, Texas 78744

Utah State Division of Wildlife Resources
1596 W. North Temple
Salt Lake City, Utah 84116

Vermont Fish and Game Department
103 S. Main Street
Waterbury, Vermont 05676

Virginia Department of Game and Inland
 Fisheries
4010 W. Broad Street, Box 11104
Richmond, Virginia 23230

Washington Department of Game
600 N. Capitol Way
Olympia, Washington 98504

West Virginia Division of Wildlife
 Resources
1800 Washington Street East
Charleston, West Virginia 25305

Wisconsin Department of Natural
  Resources
Box 7921
Madison, Wisconsin 53707

Wyoming Game and Fish Department
5400 Bishop Blvd.
Cheyenne, Wyoming 82002

Wildlife
Education Programs

National Park Service Institutes:

Canyonlands Field Institute
P.O. Box 68
Moab, Utah 84532

Glacier Institute
P.O. Box 1457
Kalispell, Montana 59903

Great Smoky Mountains Institute at
  Tremont
Great Smoky Mountains National Park
Townsend, Tennessee 37882

Lassen Field Seminars
Loomis Museum Association
P.O. Box 100
Mineral, California 96063

North Cascades Institute
2105 Highway 20
Sedro Woolley, Washington 98284

Olympic Park Institute
600 East Park Avenue
Port Angeles, Washington 98362

Point Reyes Field Seminars
Point Reyes National Seashore
Point Reyes, California 94956

Rocky Mountain Seminars
Rocky Mountain National Park
Estes Park, Colorado 80517

Sequoia Kings Canyon Seminars
Sequoia Natural History Association
Ash Mountain, Box 10
Three Rivers, California 93271

Smoky Mountain Field School
University of Tennessee
2016 Lake Avenue
Knoxville, Tennessee 37996

Teton Science School
Grand Teton National Park
P.O. Box 68
Kelly, Wyoming 83011

Waterton Heritage Education Program
Waterton Natural History Assn.
Box 145
Waterton, Alberta, Canada TOK2MO

Wildlands Research Institute
San Francisco State University
3 Mosswood Circle
Cazadero, California 95421

Yellowstone Institute
P.O. Box 117
Yellowstone Park, Wyoming 82190

Yosemite Field Seminars
Yosemite Association
P.O. Box 230
El Portal, California 95318

Pacific Northwest Seminars
c/o Mt. Rainier National Park
Longmire, Washington 98397

National Wildlife Education Programs:

American Nature Study Society
5881 Cold Brook Road
Homer, New York 13077

Appalachian Mountain Club
5 Joy Street
Boston, Massachusetts 02108

Audubon Naturalist Society of the Central
  Atlantic States
8940 Jones Mill Road
Chevy Chase, Maryland 20815

Boone and Crockett Club
241 S. Fraley Blvd.
Dumfries, Virginia 22026

Boy Scouts of America—National Office
1325 Walnut Hill Lane
Irving, Texas 75038-3096

Center for Environmental Education, Inc.
1725 DeSales Street, N.W.
Washington, D.C. 20036

Defenders of Wildlife
1244 19th Street, N.W.
Washington, D.C. 20036

Elderhostel, Inc.
80 Boylston Street
Boston, Massachusetts 02116

Elsa Clubs of America
3201 Tepusquet Canyon Road
Santa Maria, California 93454

Fund for Animals, Inc.
200 W. 57th Street
New York City, New York 10019

Girl Scouts of United States of America
830 3rd Avenue
New York City, New York 10022

Hawk Mountain Sanctuary Association
R.D. #2
Kempton, Pennsylvania 19529

Humane Society of United States
2100 L Street, N.W.
Washington, D.C. 20037

International Council for Outdoor
   Education
P.O. Box 17255
Pittsburgh, Pennsylvania 15235

National Audubon Society
Education Division
Route 1, Box 171
Sharon, Connecticut 06069

National Fish and Wildlife Foundation
18th and C Streets, N.W.
Room 2626
Washington, D.C. 20240

National Institute for Urban Wildlife
10921 Trotting Ridge Way
Columbia, Maryland 21044-2831

National Wildlife Federation
1412 Sixteenth Street, N.W.
Washington, D.C. 20036-2266

The Nature Conservancy
1800 North Kent Street, Suite 800
Arlington, Virginia 22209

Smithsonian Institution
1000 Jefferson Drive, S.W.
Washington, D.C. 20560

Student Conservation Association, Inc.
Box 550
Charlestown, New Hampshire 03603

Welder Wildlife Foundation
P.O. Box 1400
Sinton, Texas 78387

Wildlife Information Center, Inc.
629 Green Street
Allentown, Pennsylvania 18102

The Wildlife Society
5410 Grosvenor Lane
Bethesda, Maryland 20814

Index

*Some other fine nature books
from America's Great Outdoor Publisher*

Basic Projects in Wildlife Watching
Experience the world of wildlife more closely with over two dozen projects, including sharpening your senses, making yourself invisible to wildlife, detecting predators, and calling birds.
by Sam Fadala

Ruffed Grouse
The complete and compelling story of the ruffed grouse, told by 27 wildlife biologists. Beautifully illustrated with full-color art and photography.

Wildlife Management on Your Land
The practical owner's manual for habitat improvements.
by Charles L. Cadieux

The Deer of North America
The definitive book on North American deer by one of the world's leading photojournalists.
by Leonard Lee Rue III

Animal Tracks and Signs of North America
A detailed, illustrated field guide for identifying all kinds of wildlife signs.
by Richard P. Smith

Bear in Their World
A lavishly illustrated book on black bears, grizzlies, brown bears, and polar bears.
by Erwin A. Bauer

Soft Paths
How to enjoy the wilderness without harming it.
by Bruce Hampton and David Cole

*Available at your local bookstore,
or for complete ordering information, write:*

**Stackpole Books
P.O. Box 1831
Cameron and Kelker Streets
Harrisburg, PA 17105**

For faster service, credit card users may call 1-800-READ-NOW
In Pennsylvania, call 717-234-5041